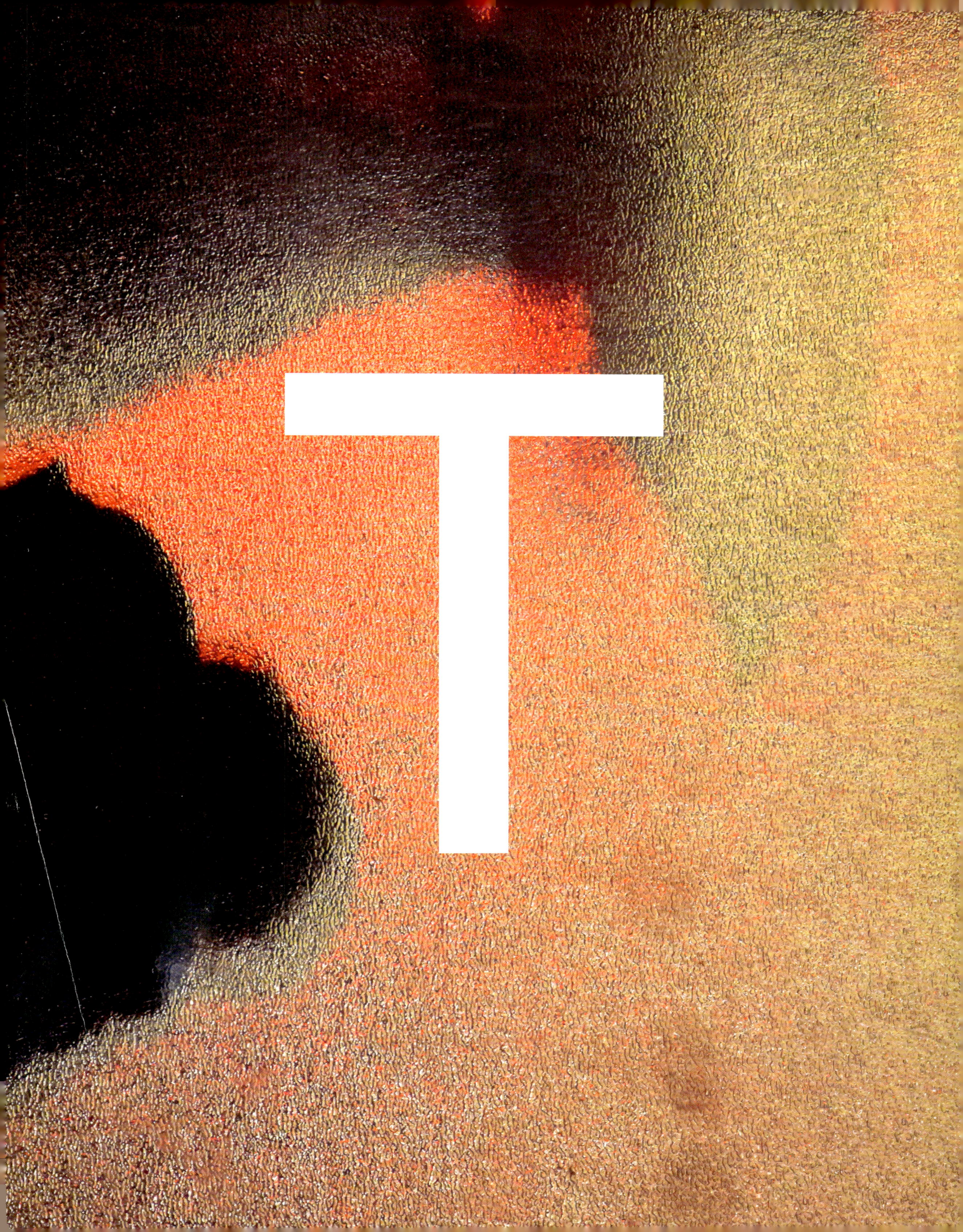
T

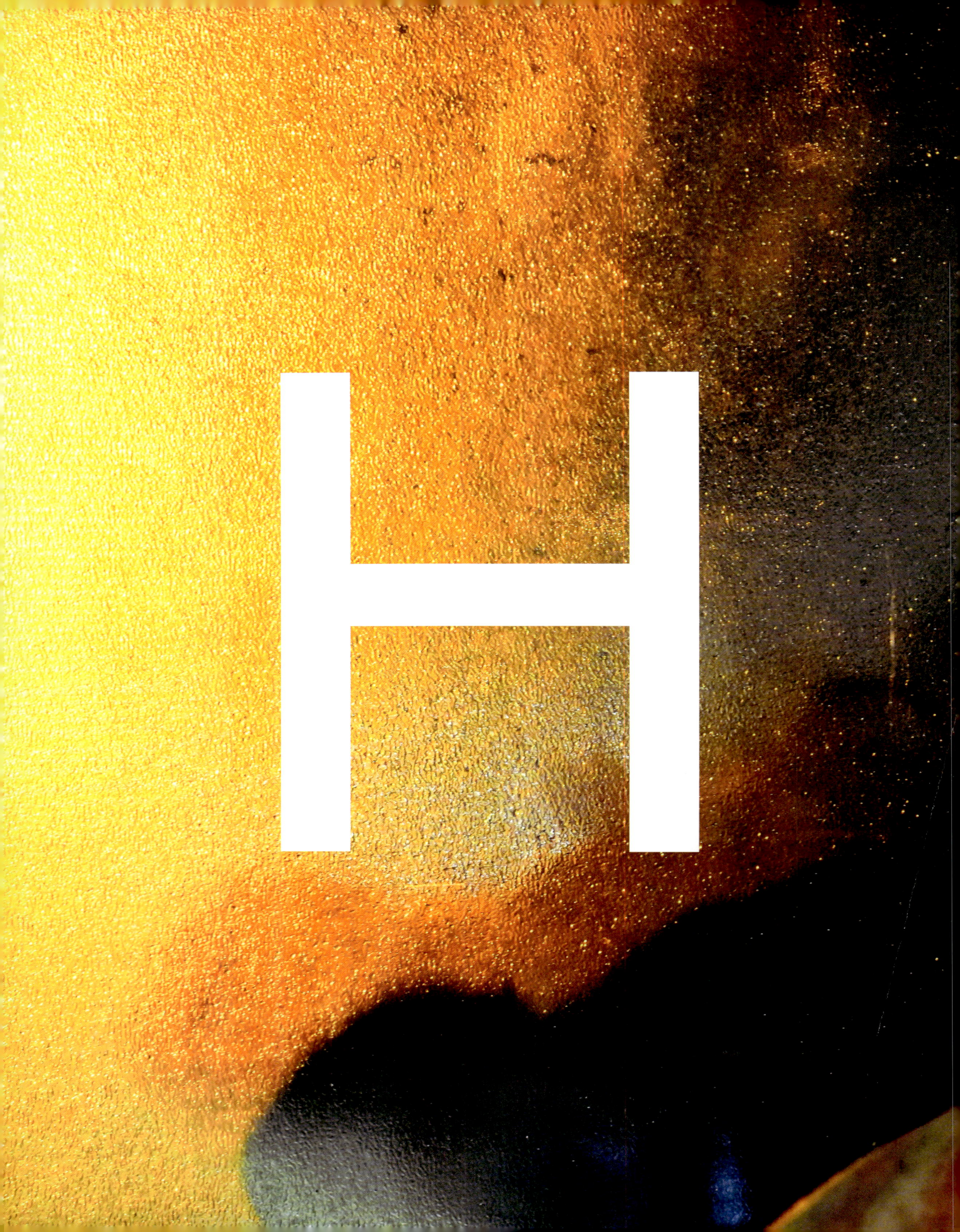
H

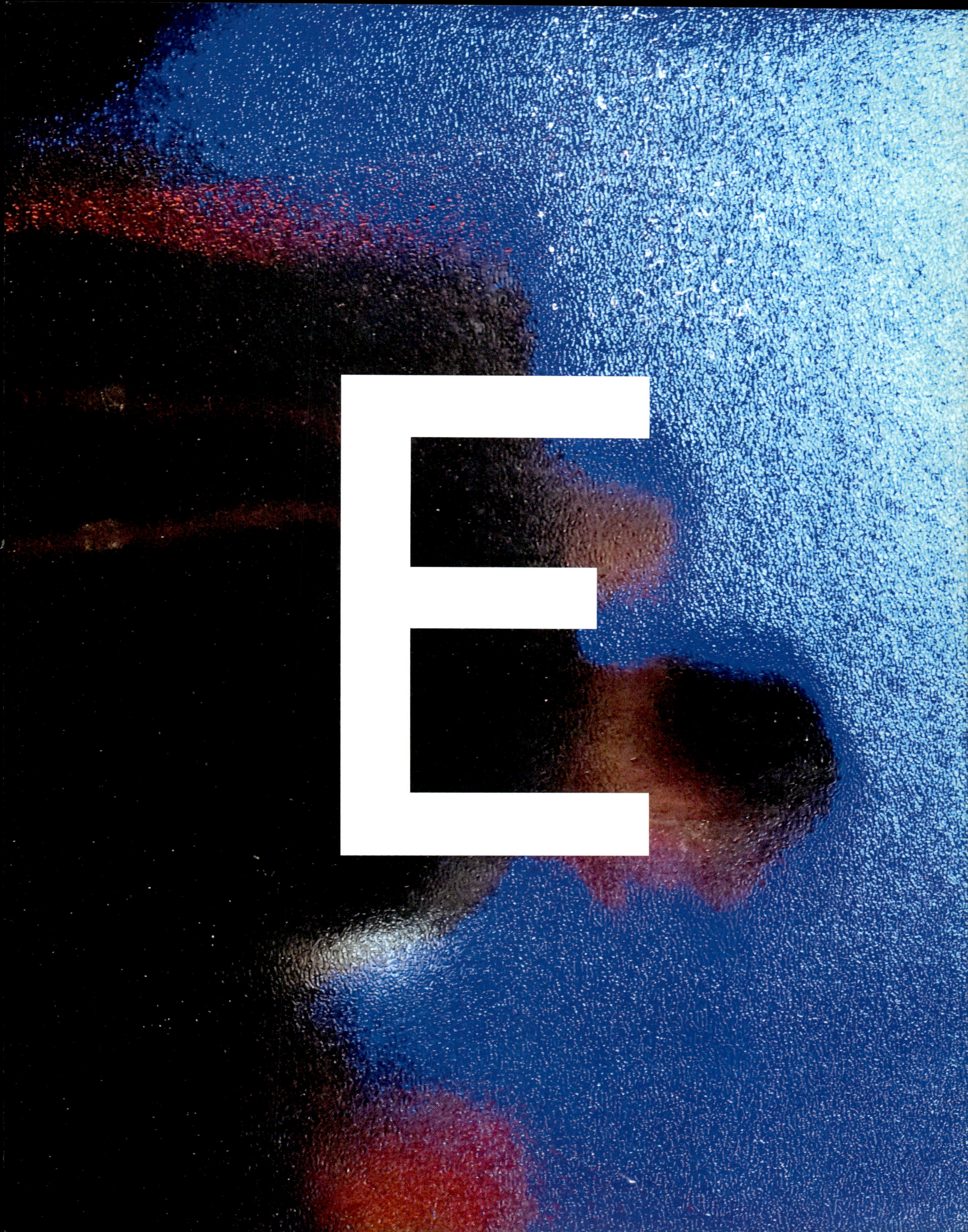
E

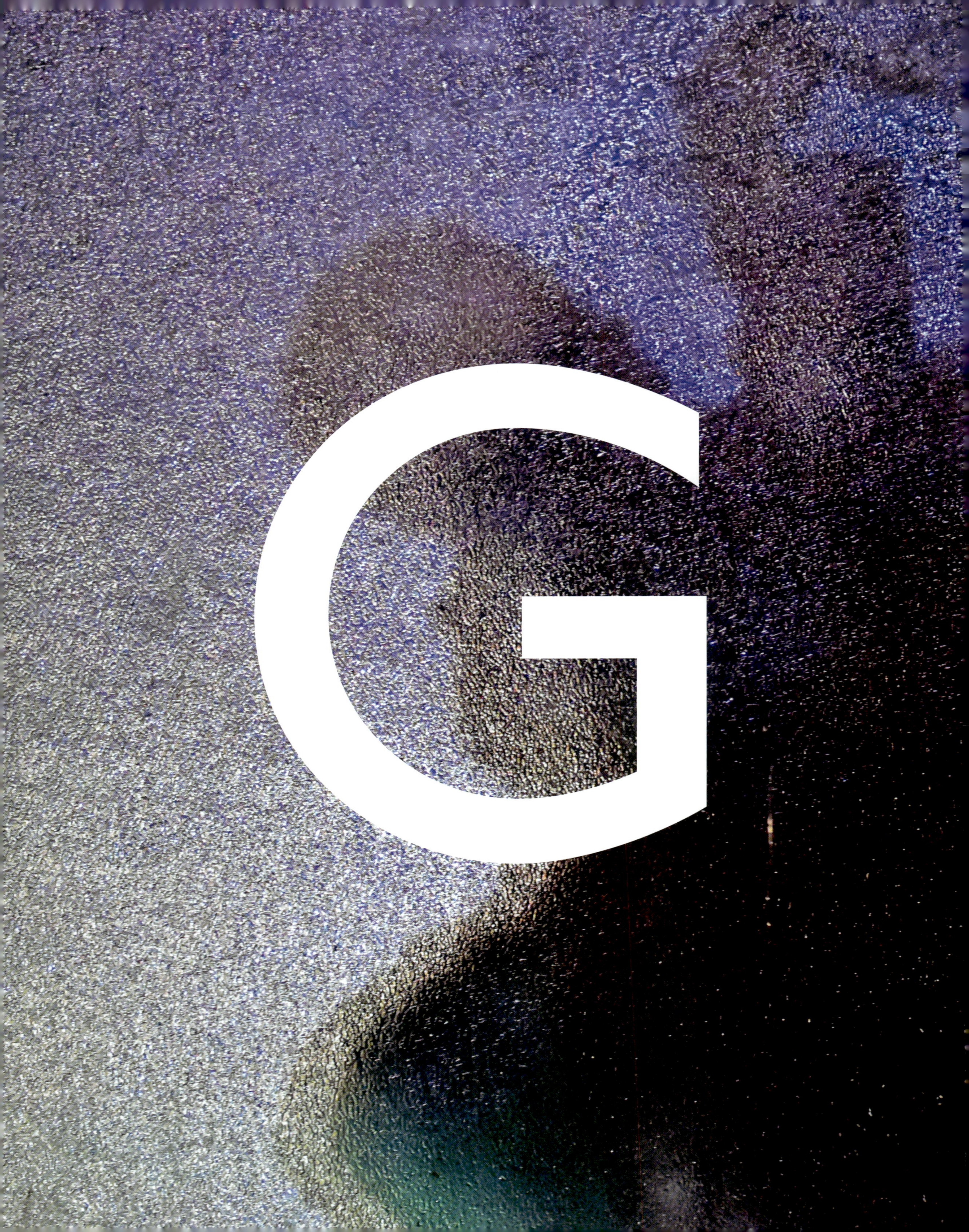
G

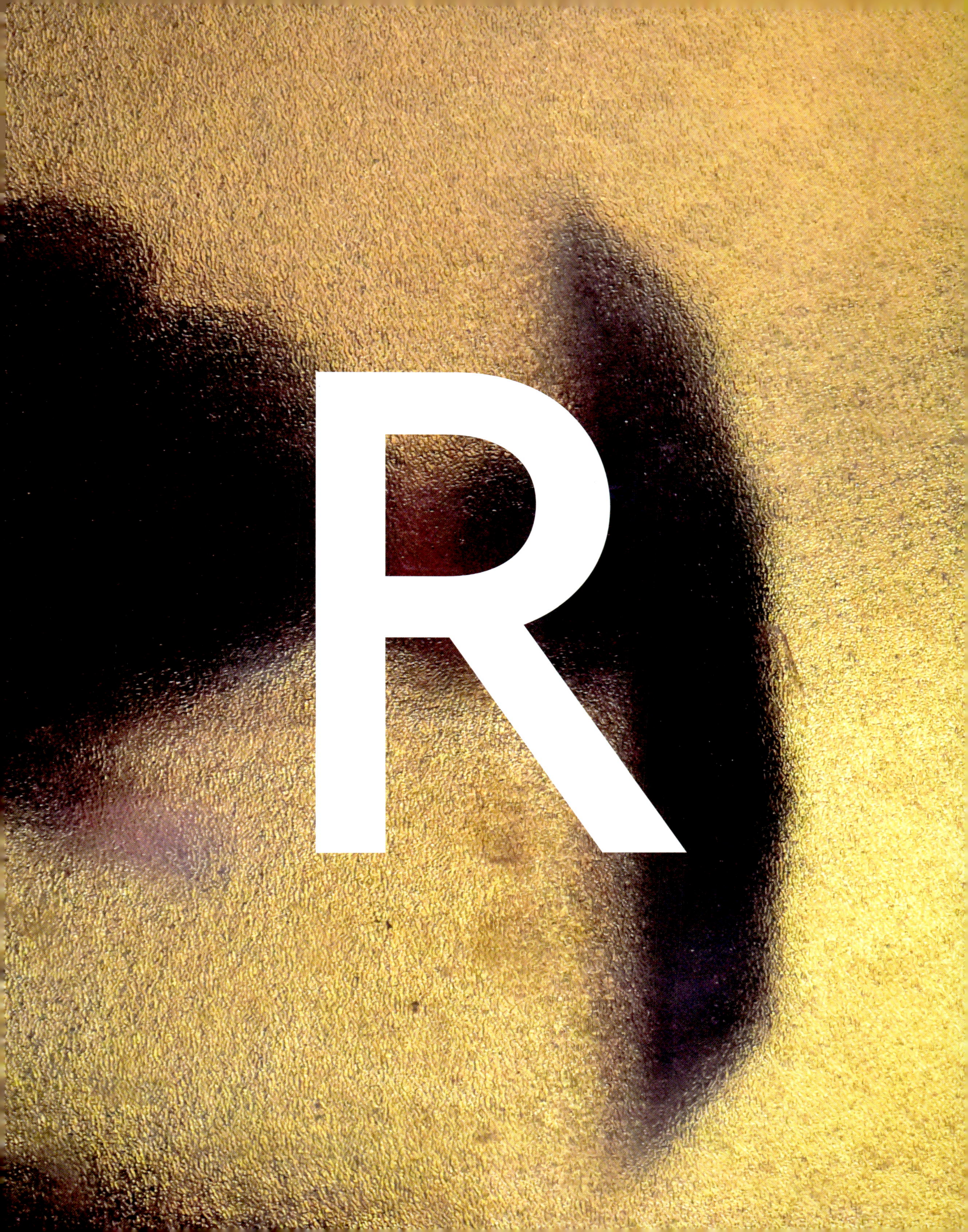
R

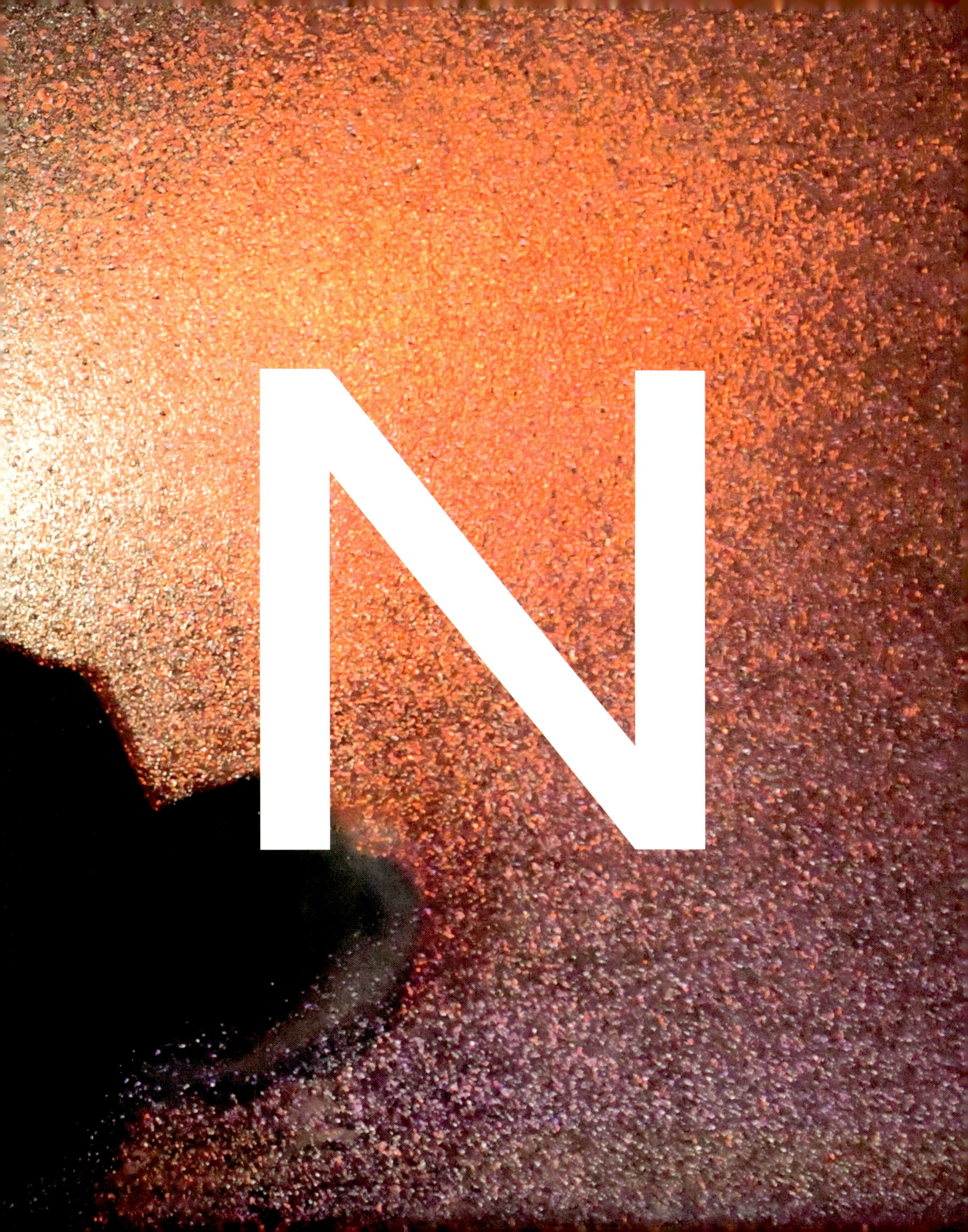
N

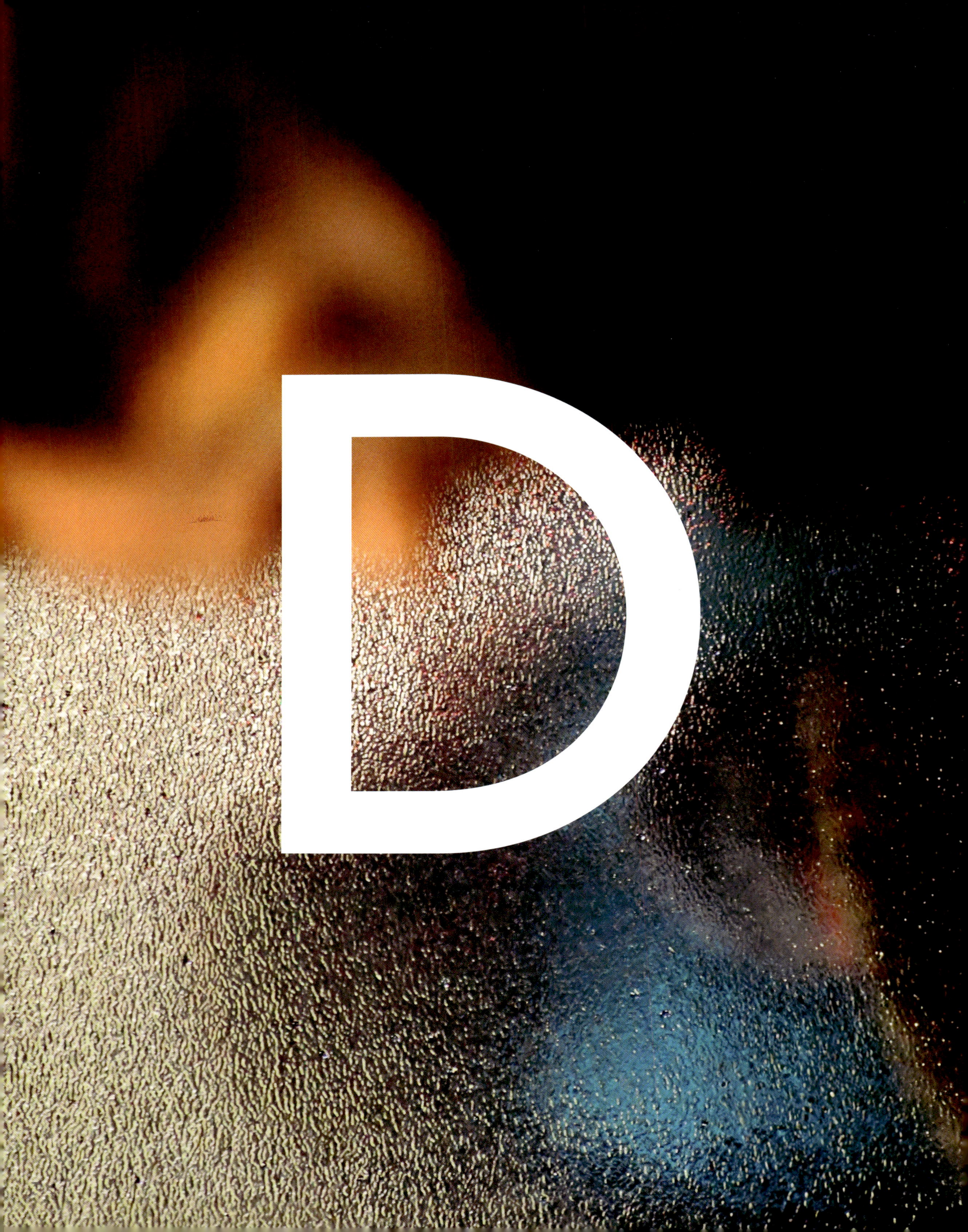
D

Steve Madden

THE GRIND

GOST

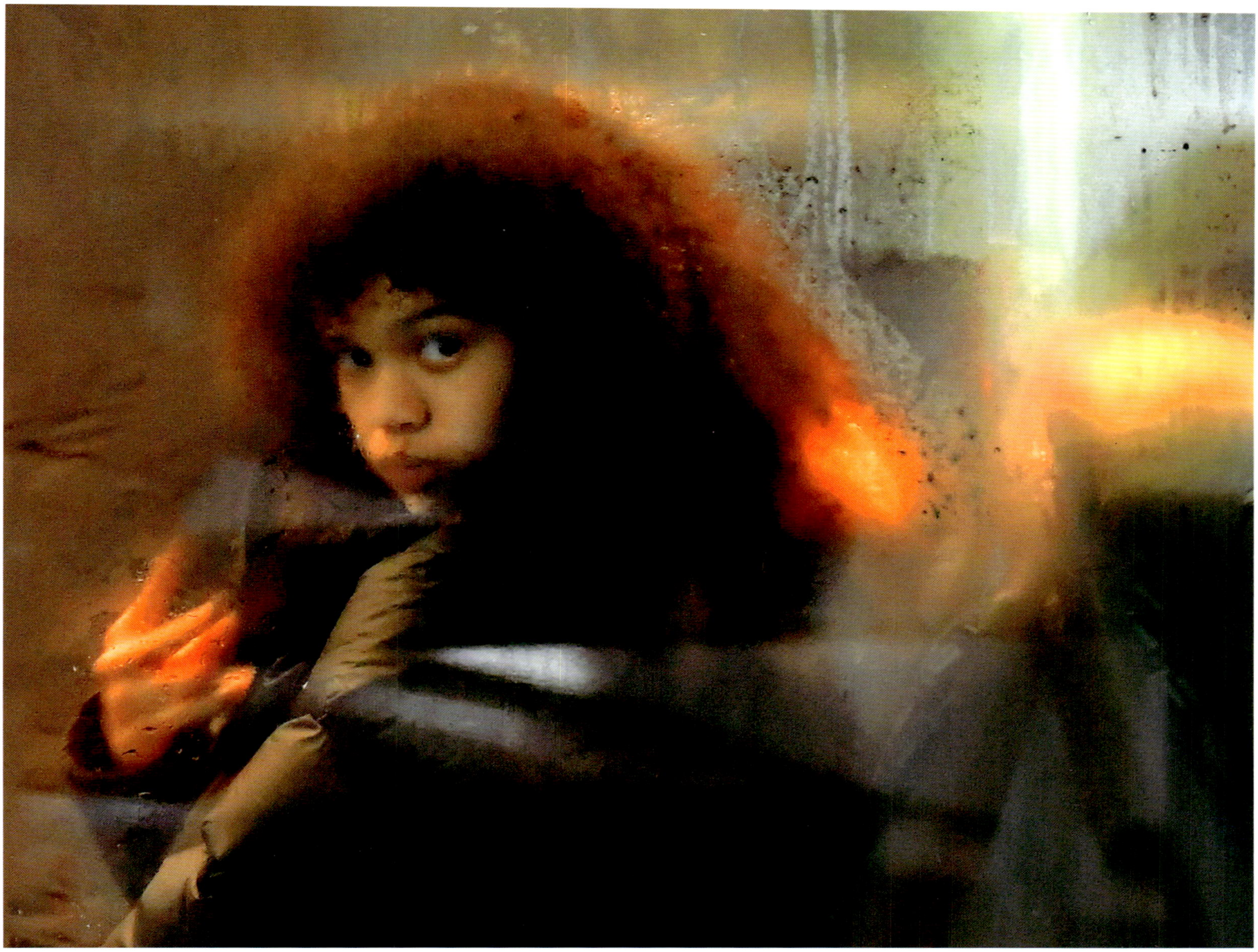

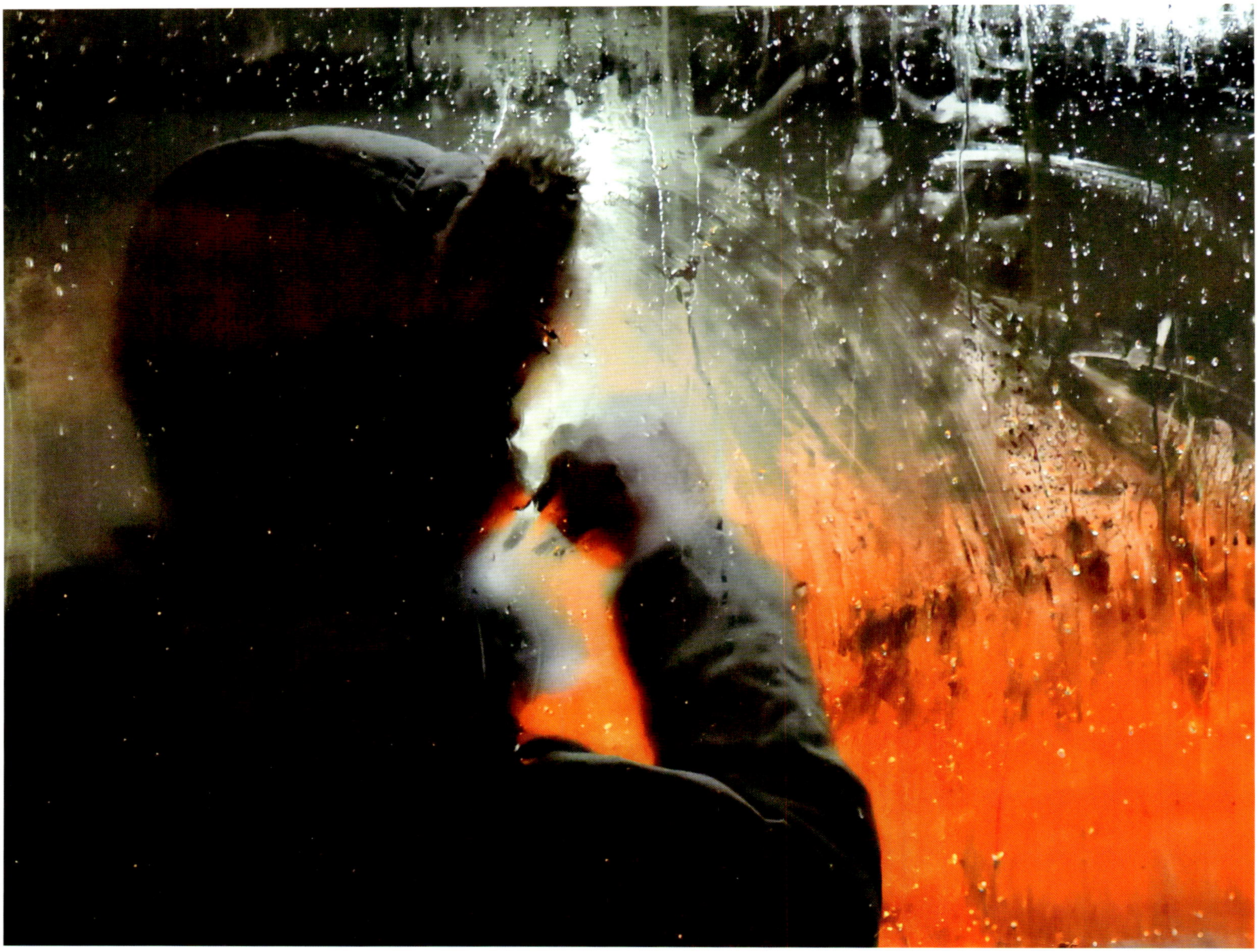

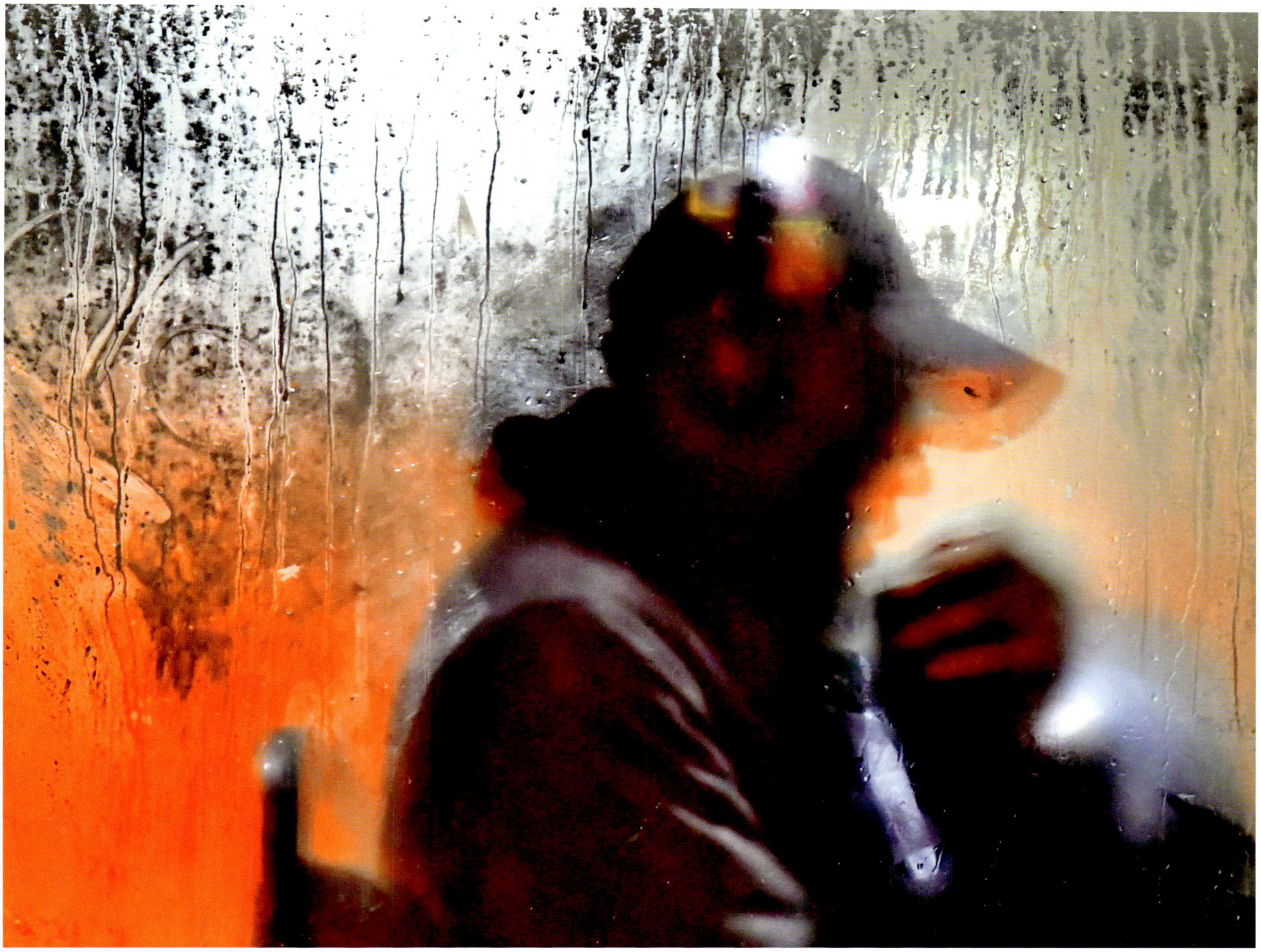

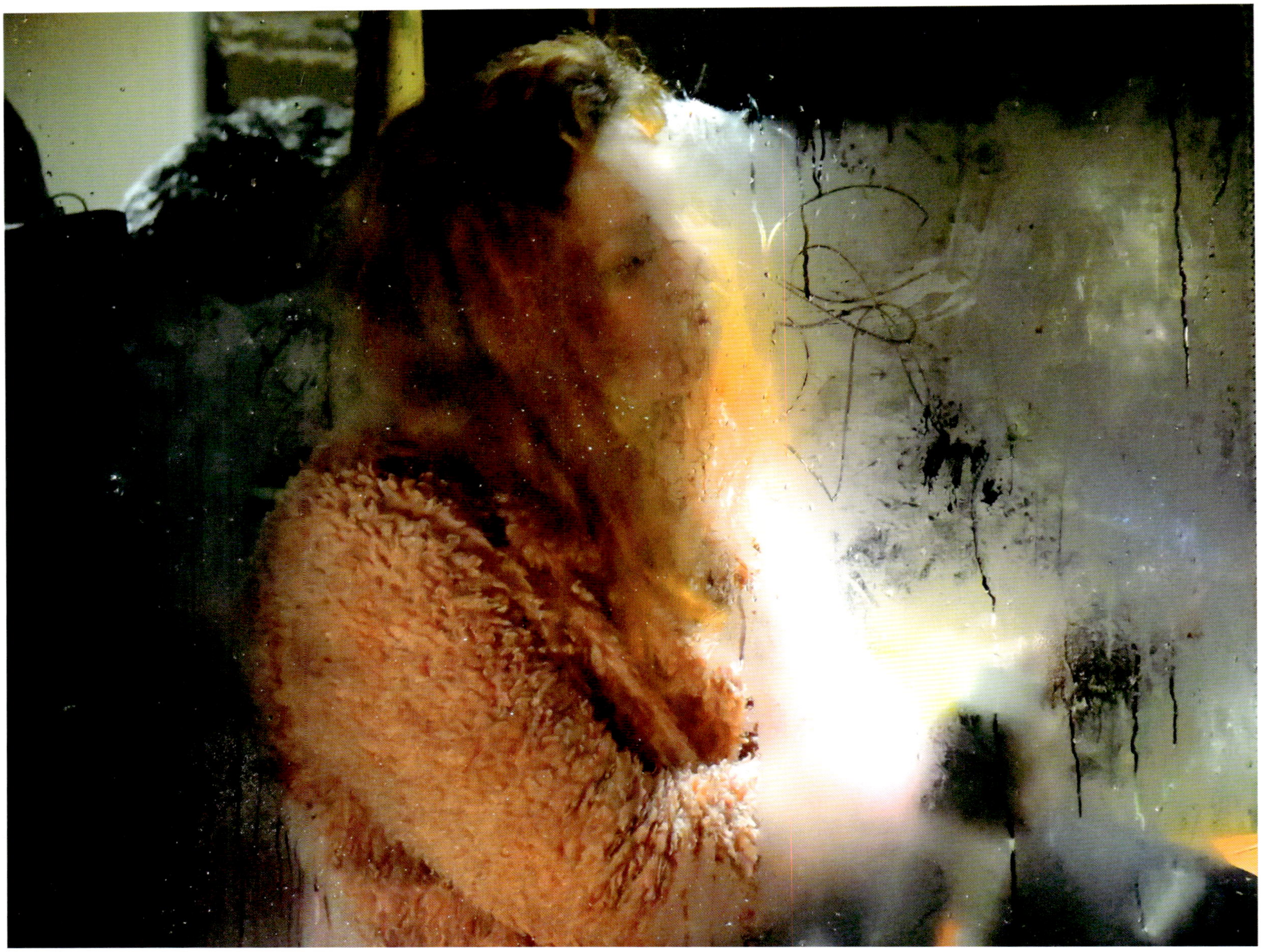

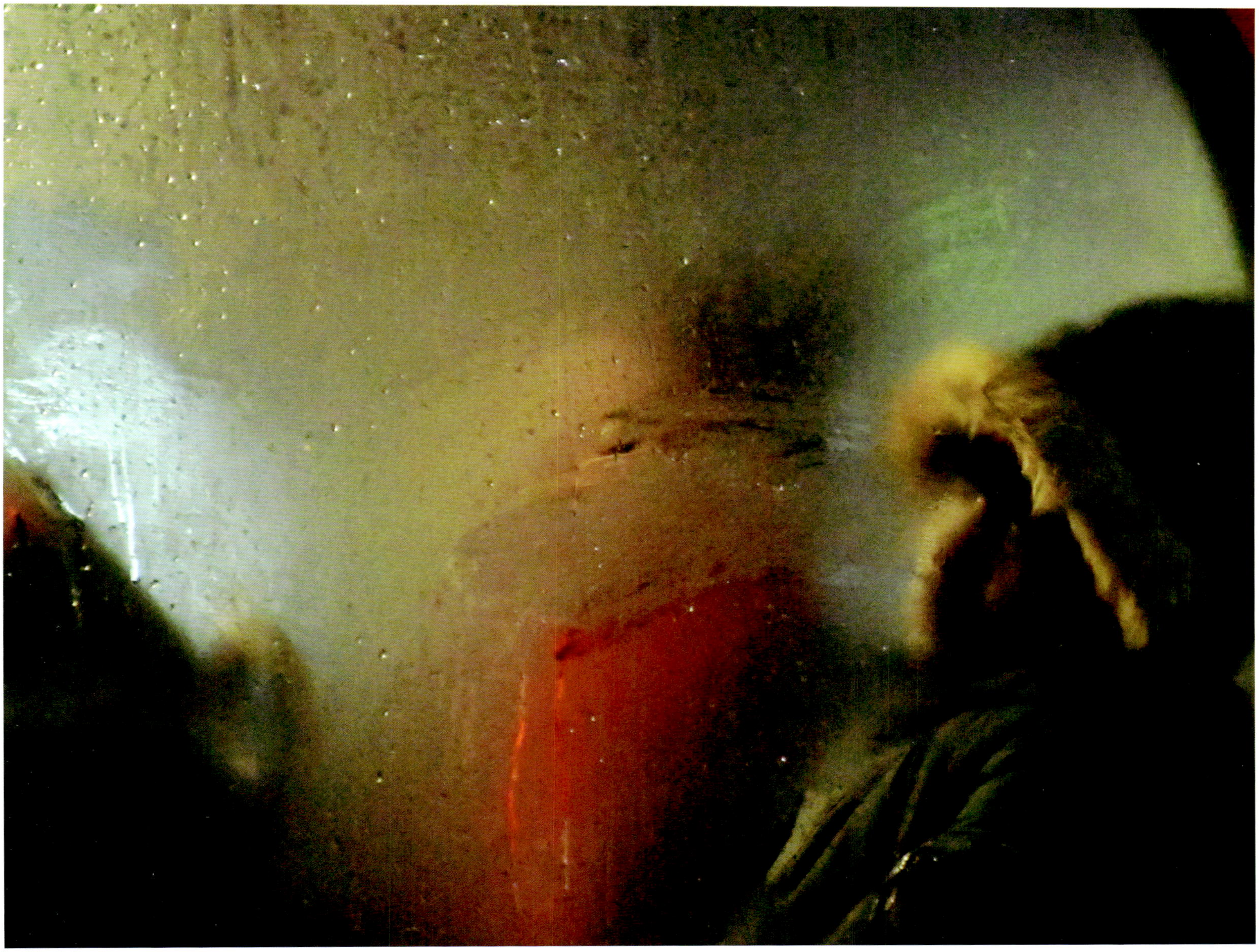

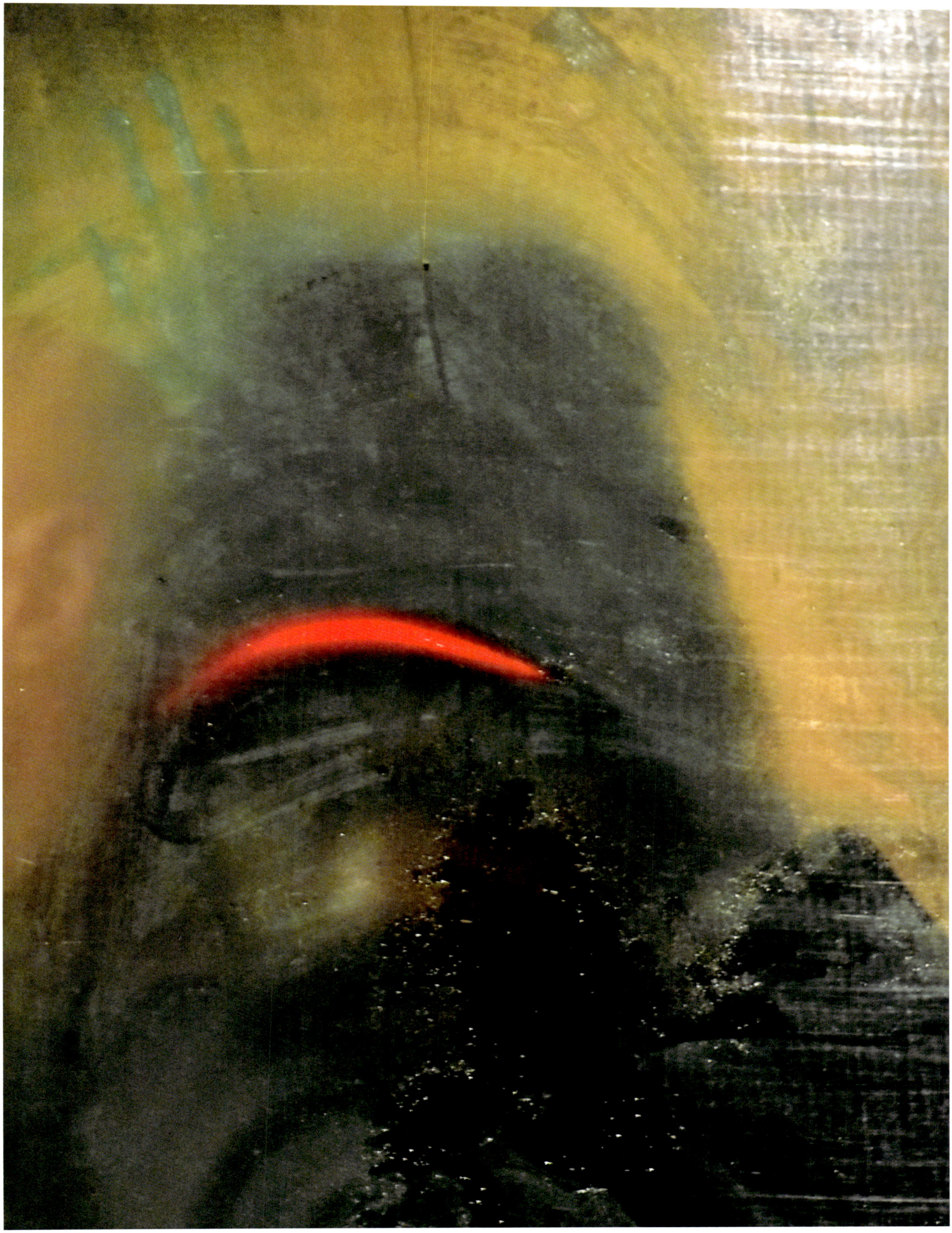

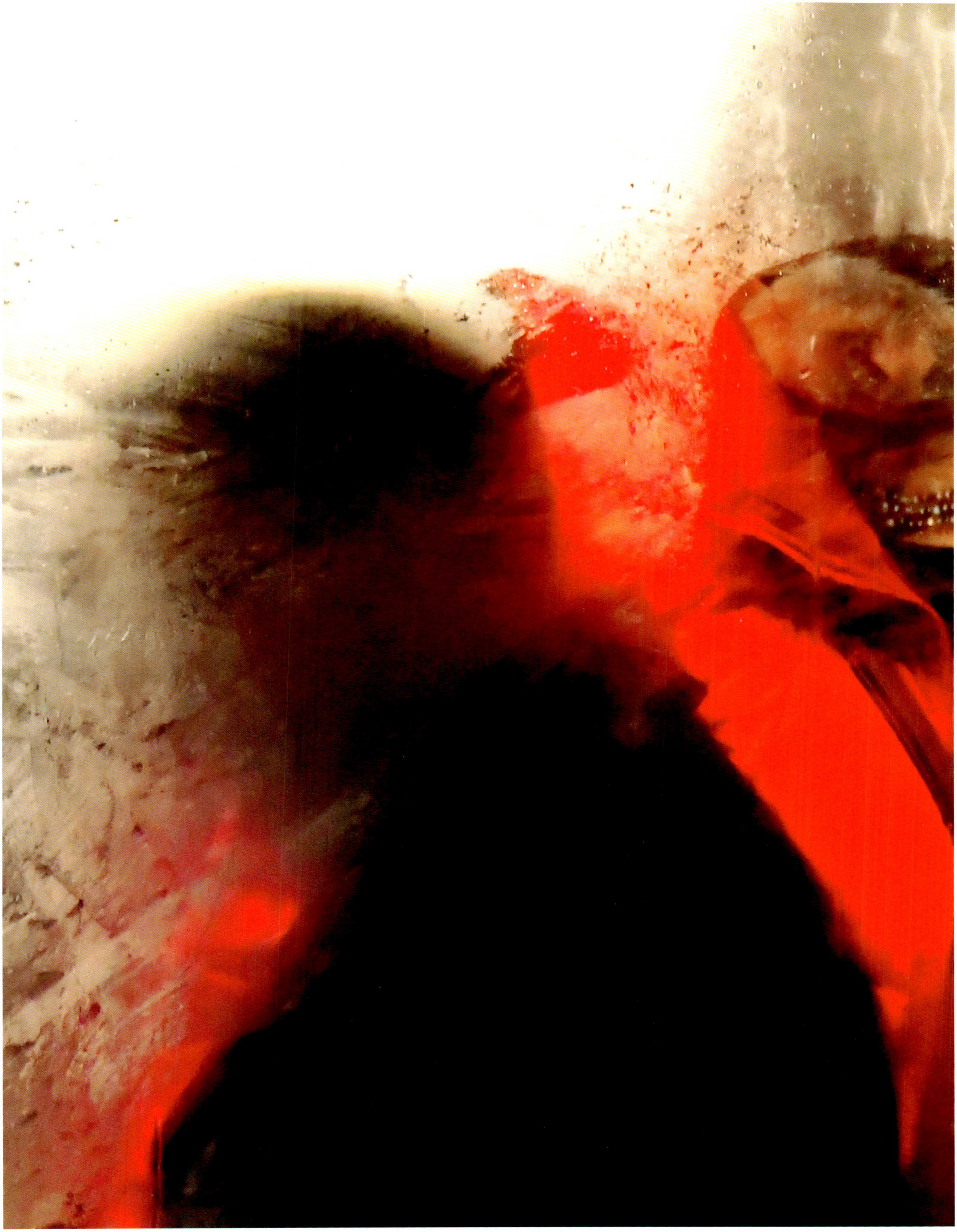

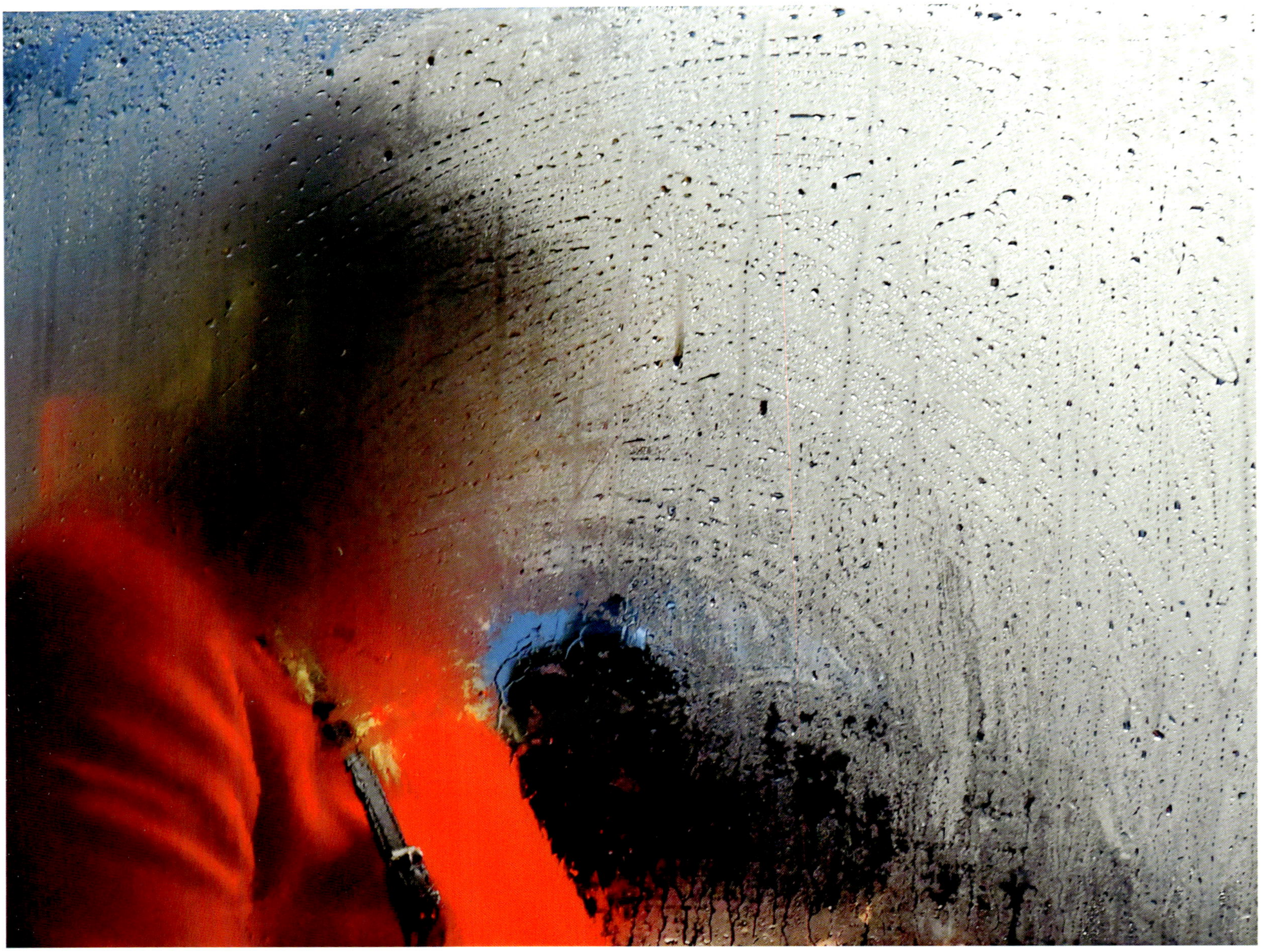

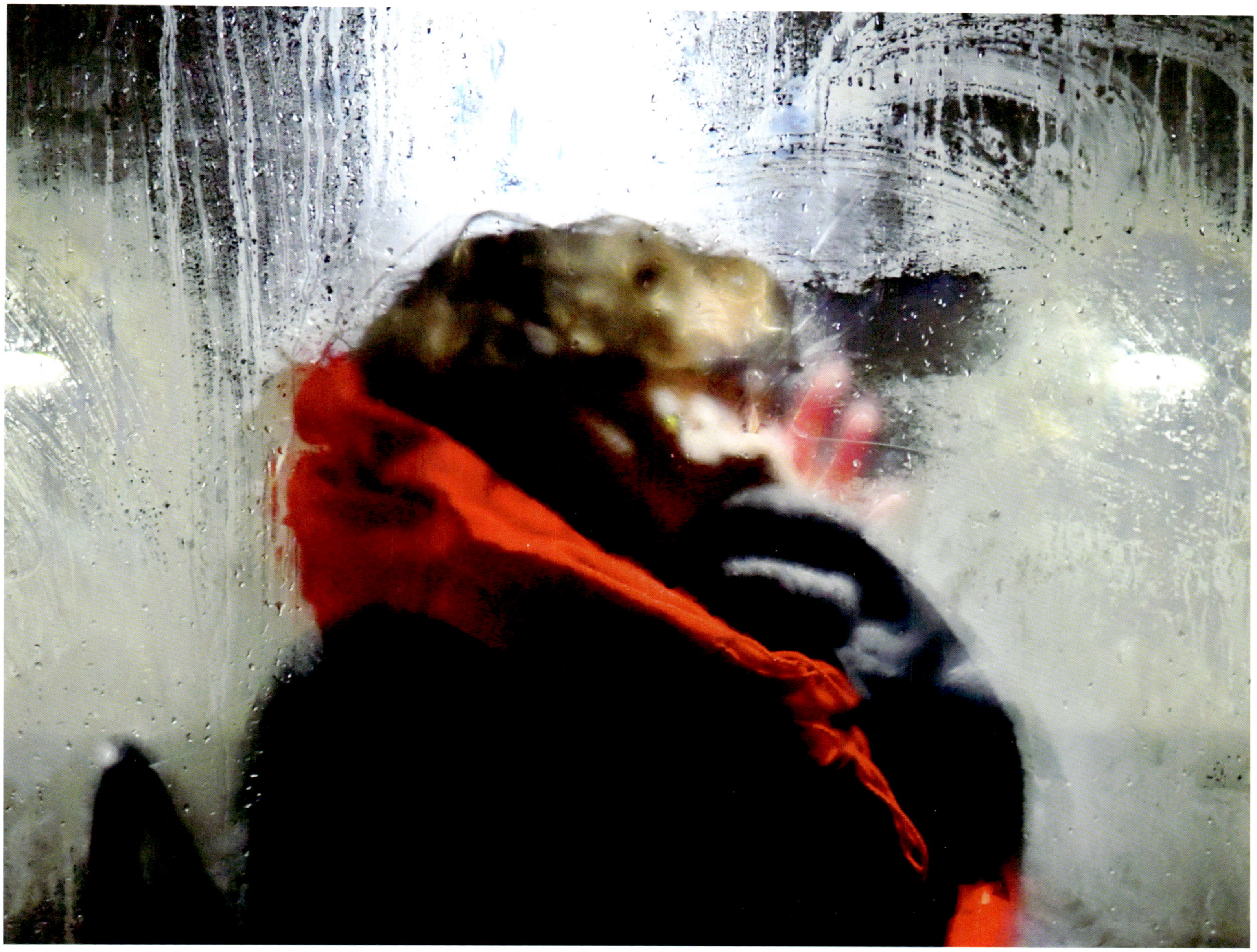

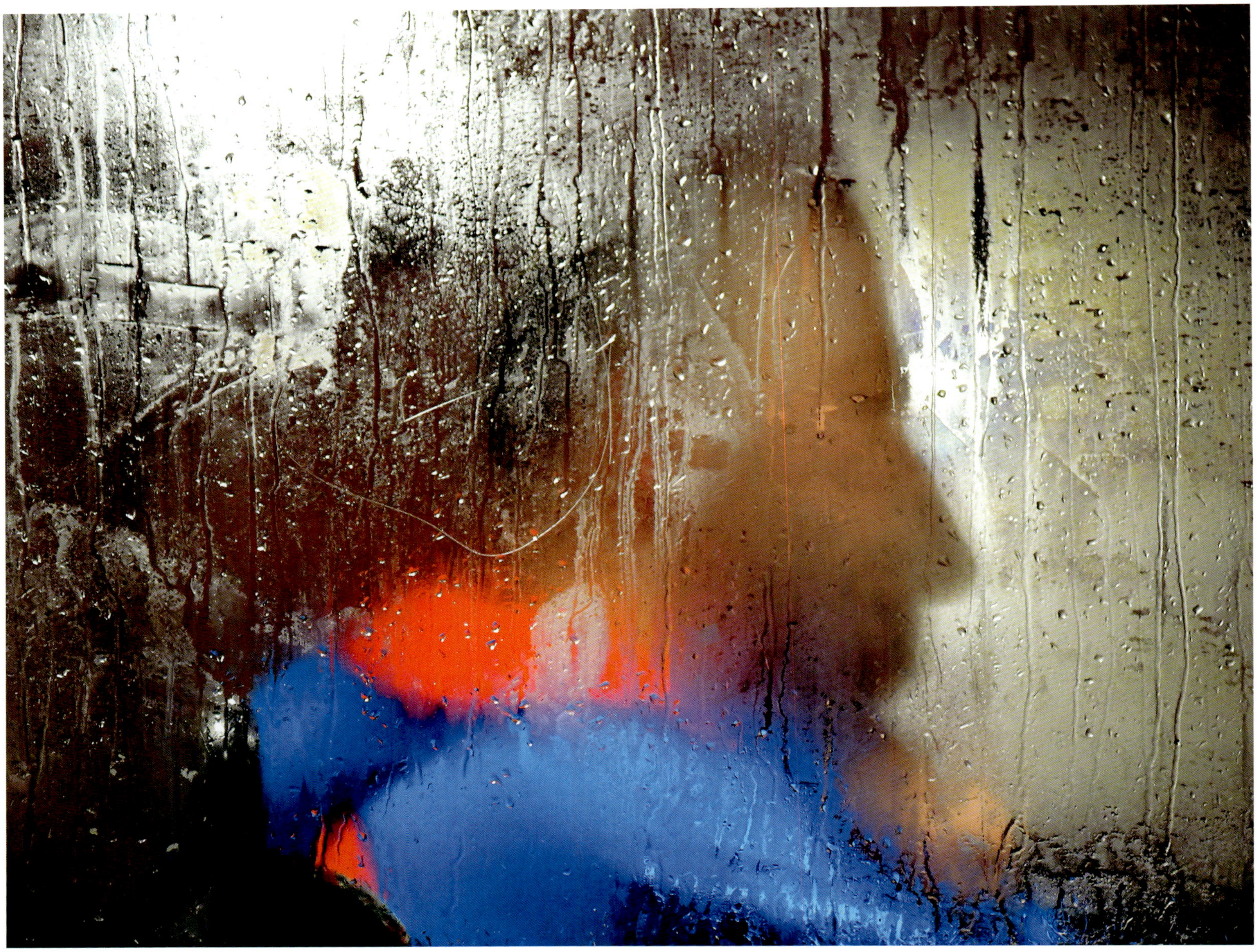

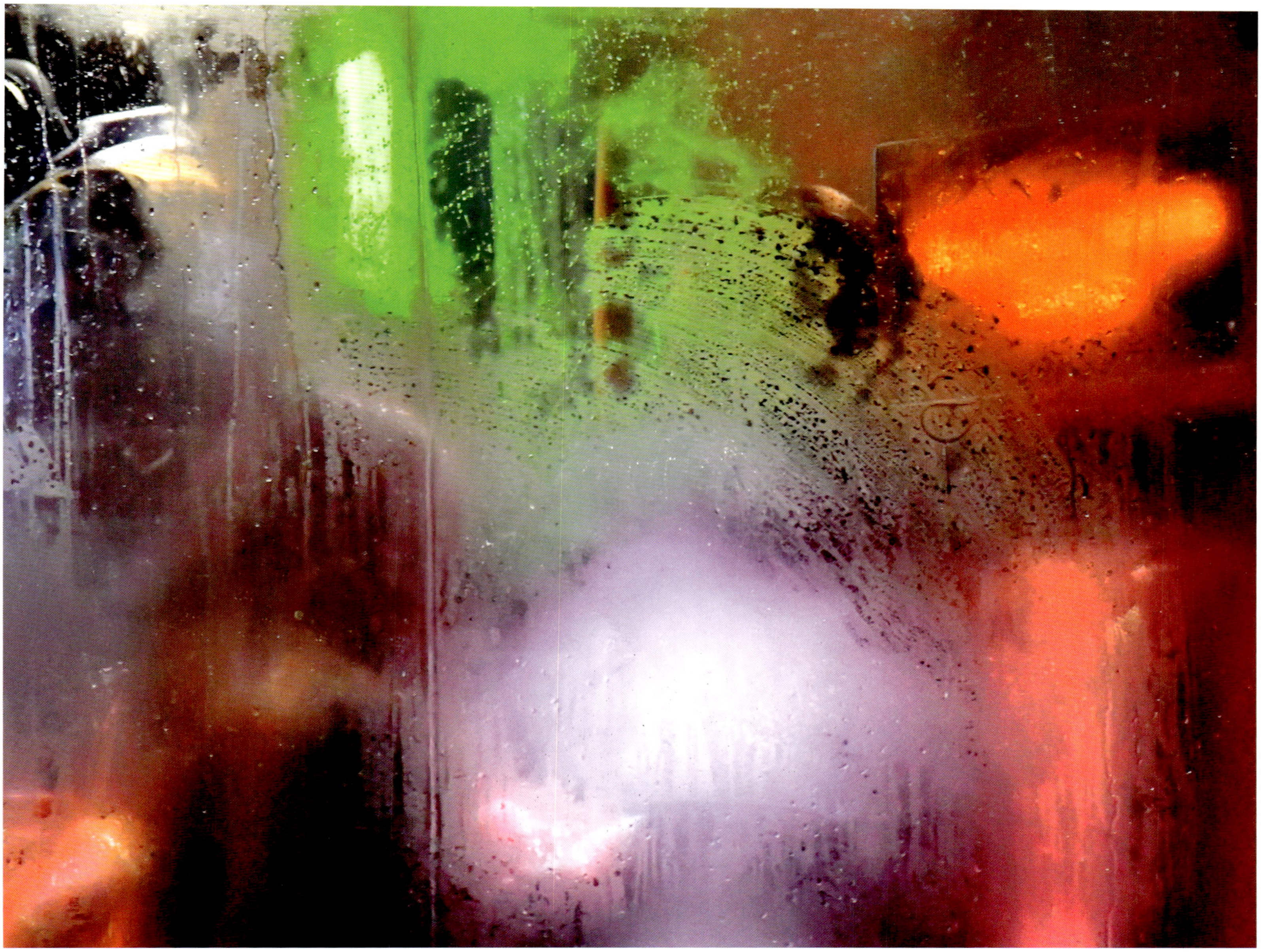

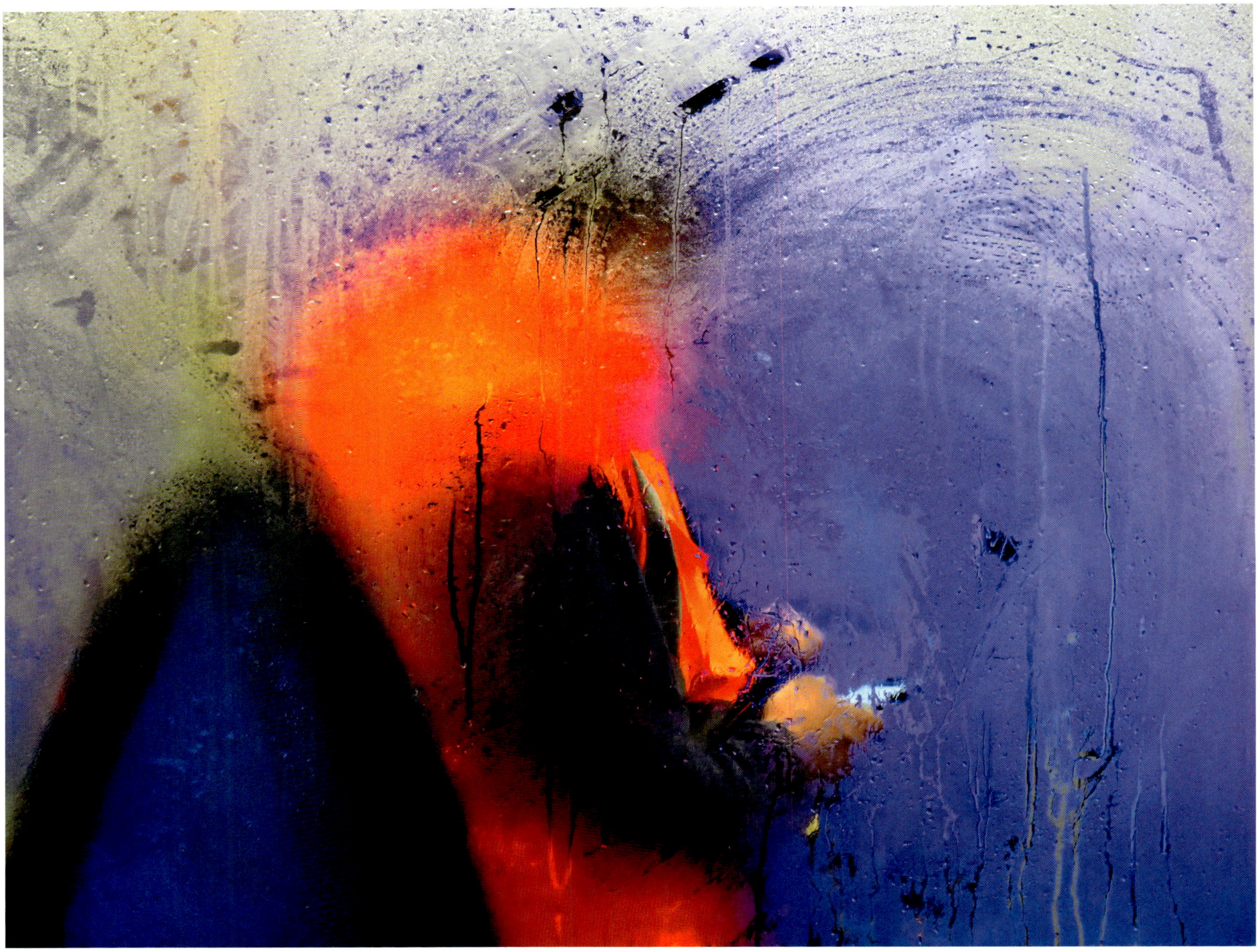

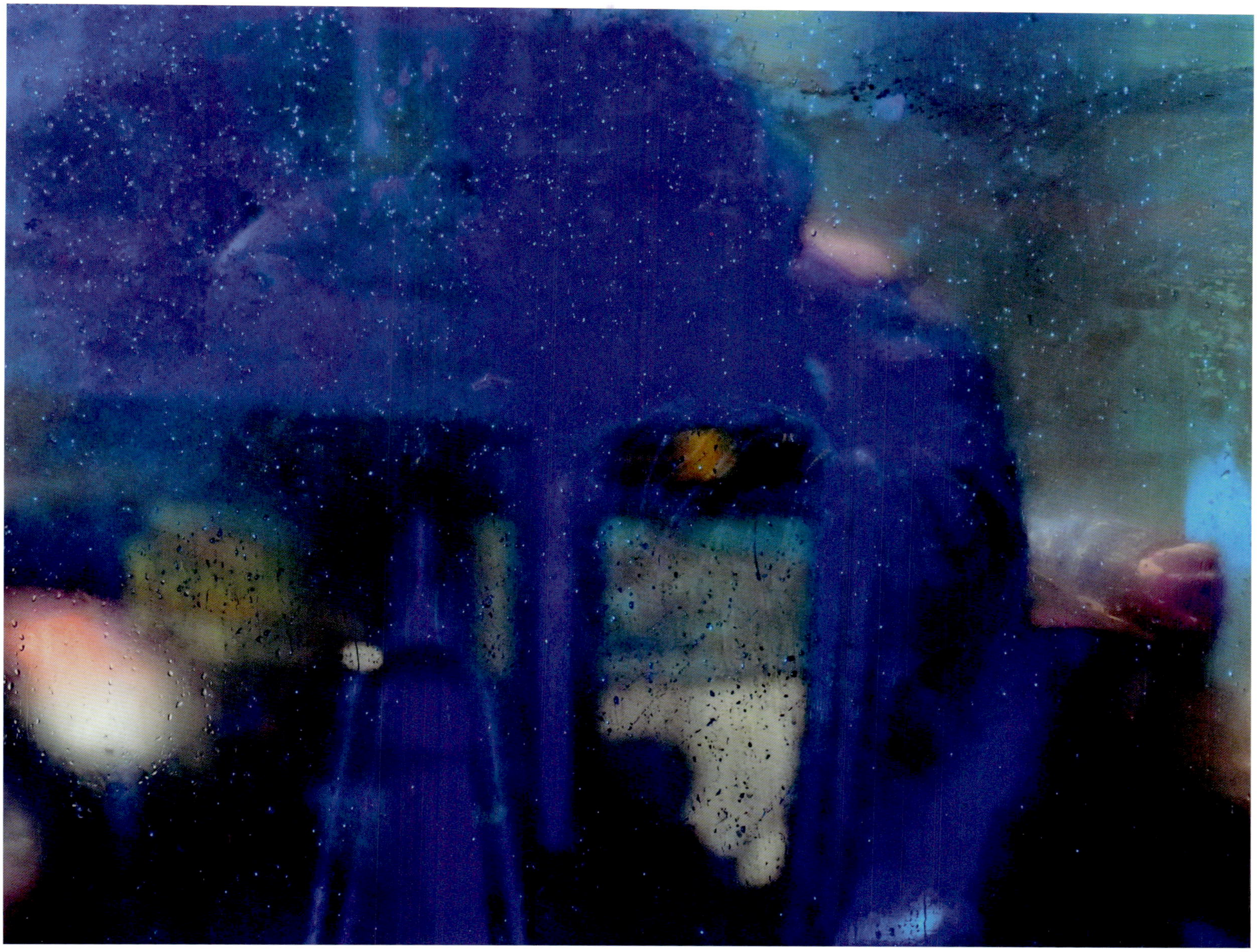

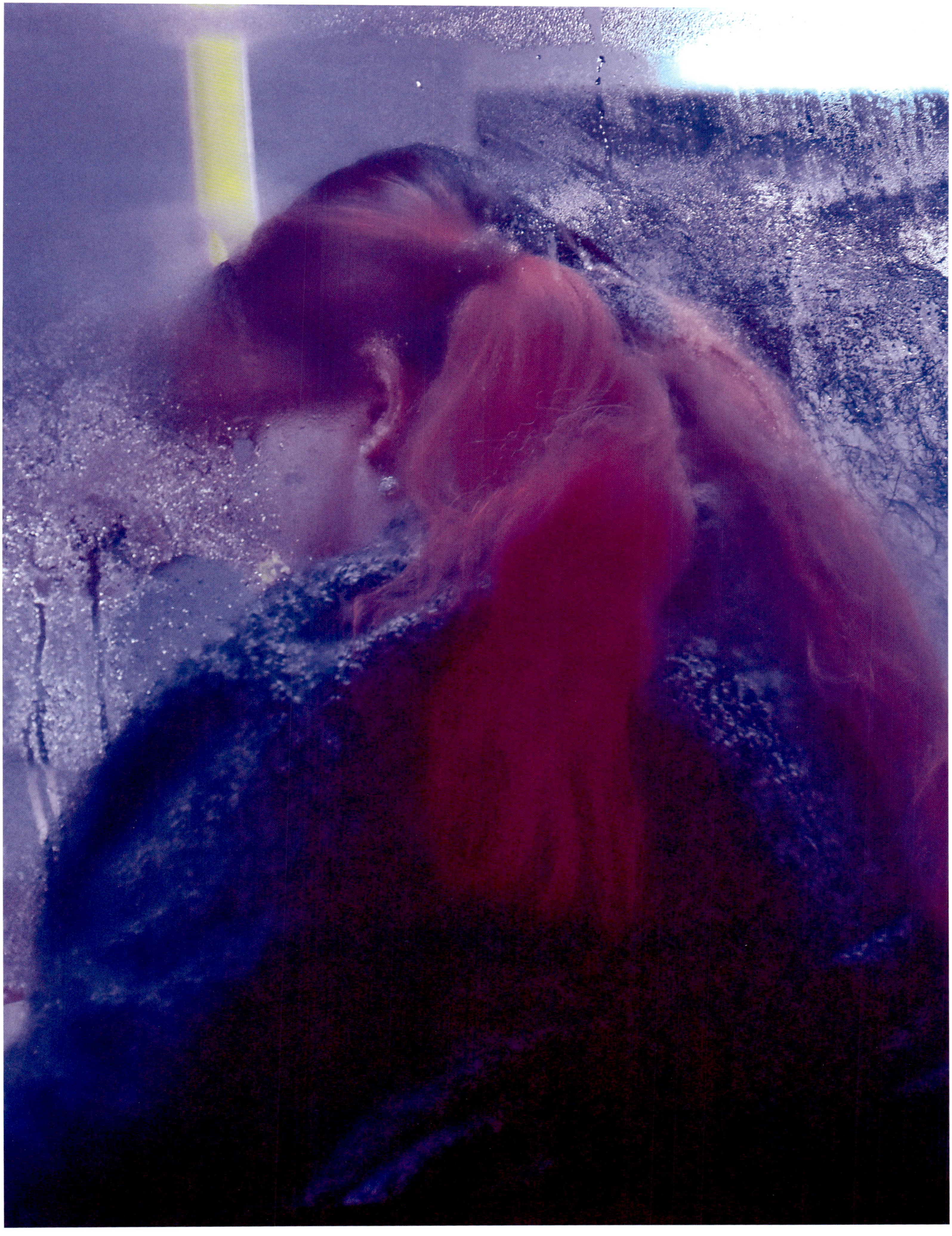

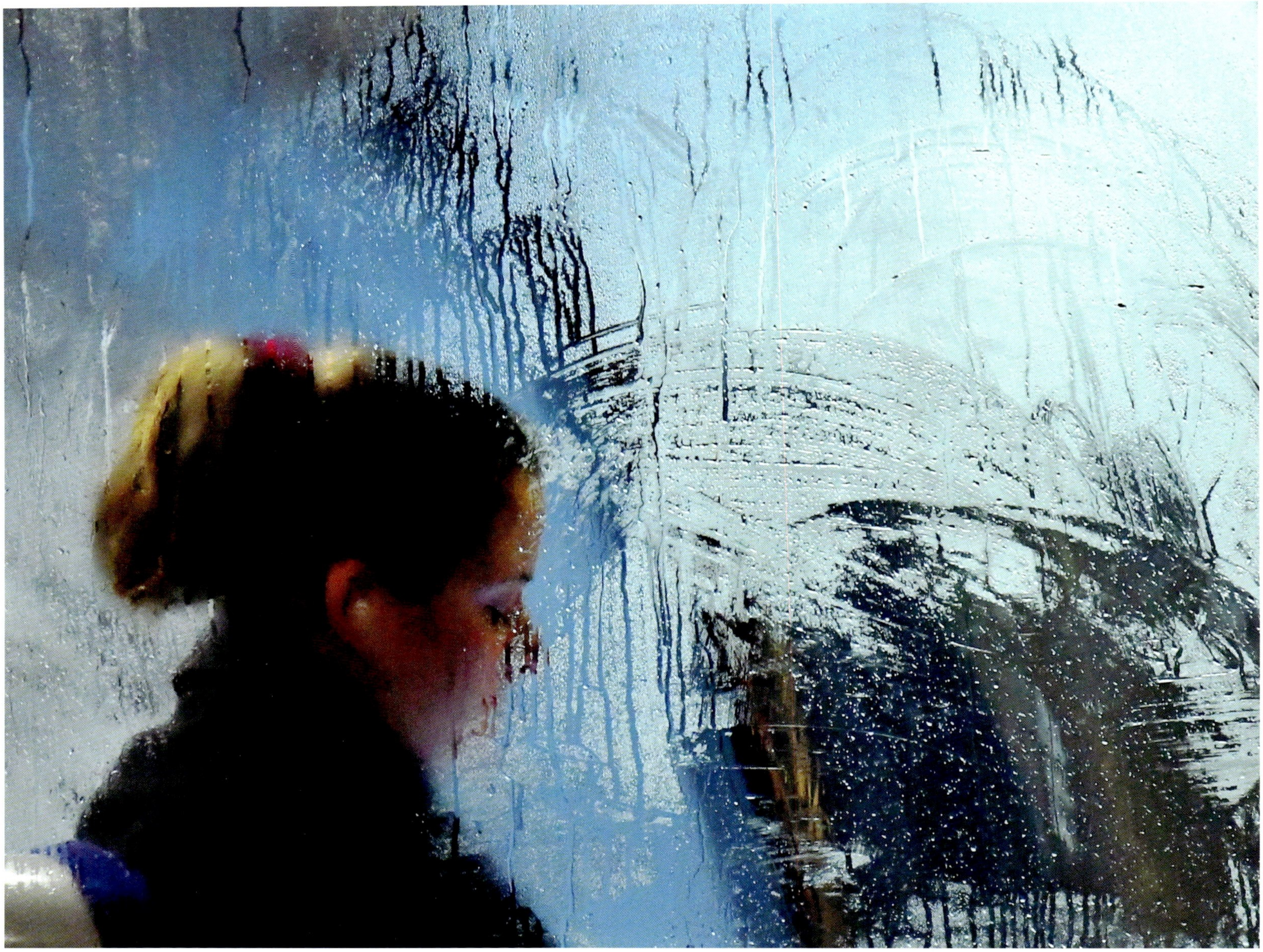

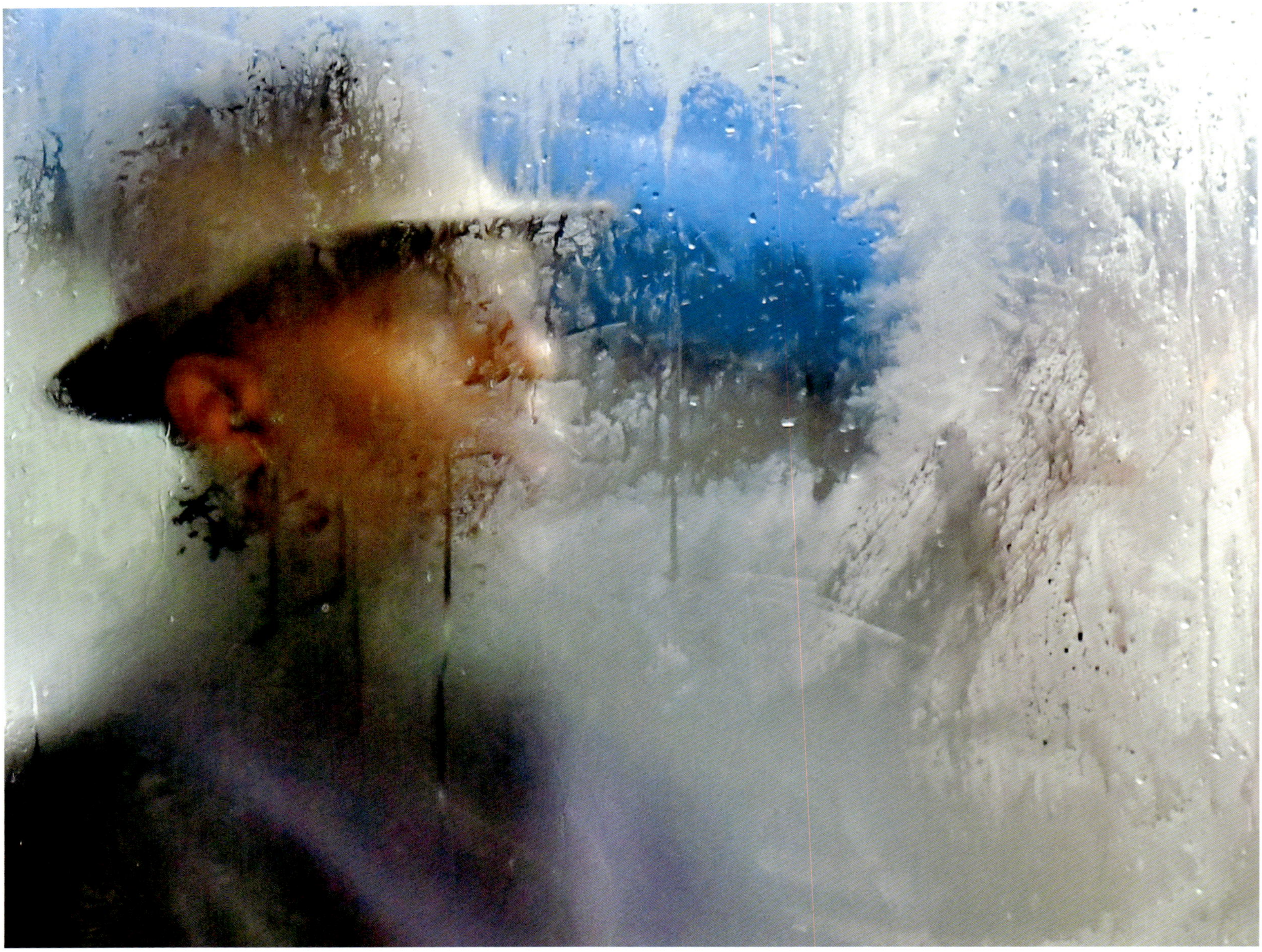

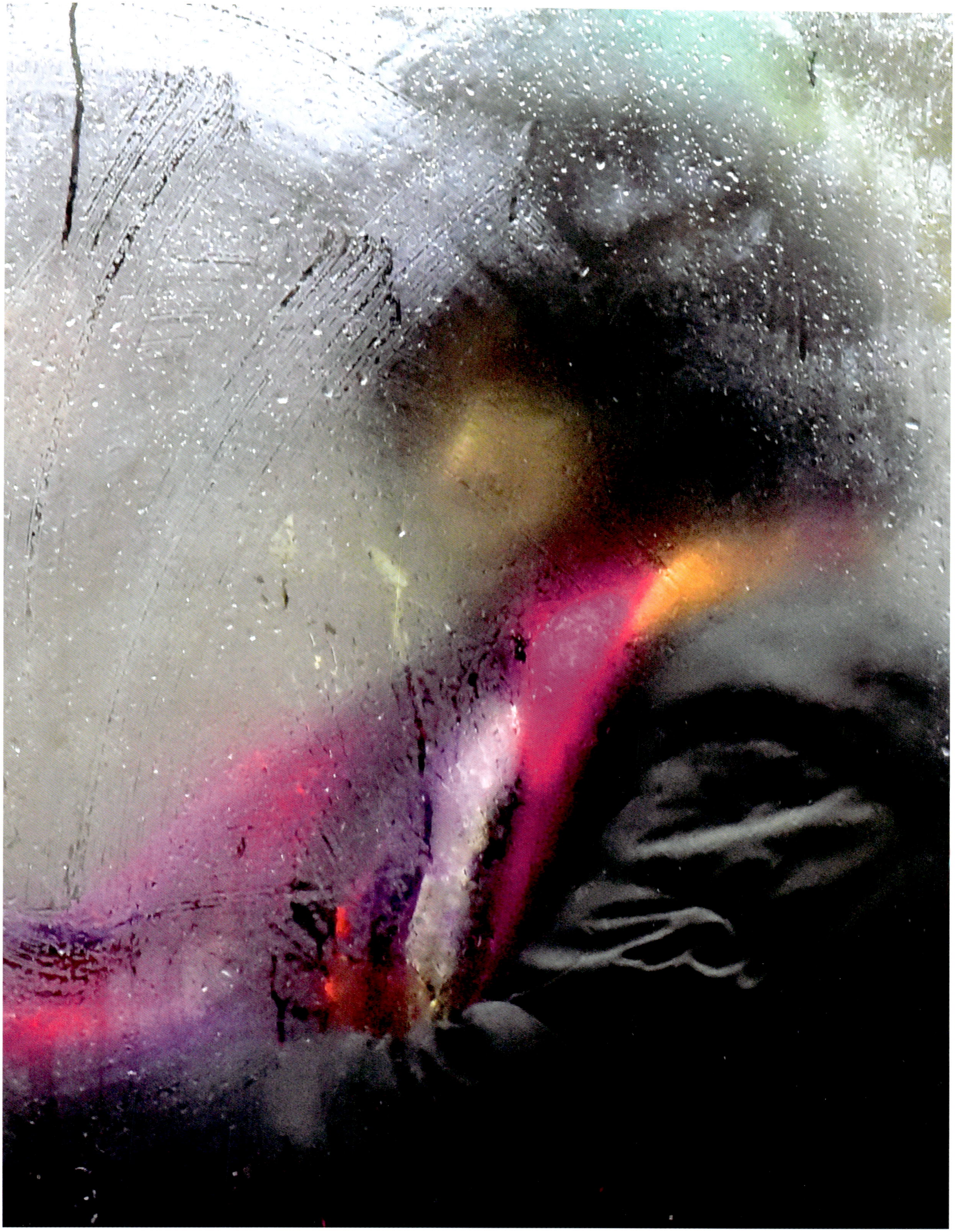

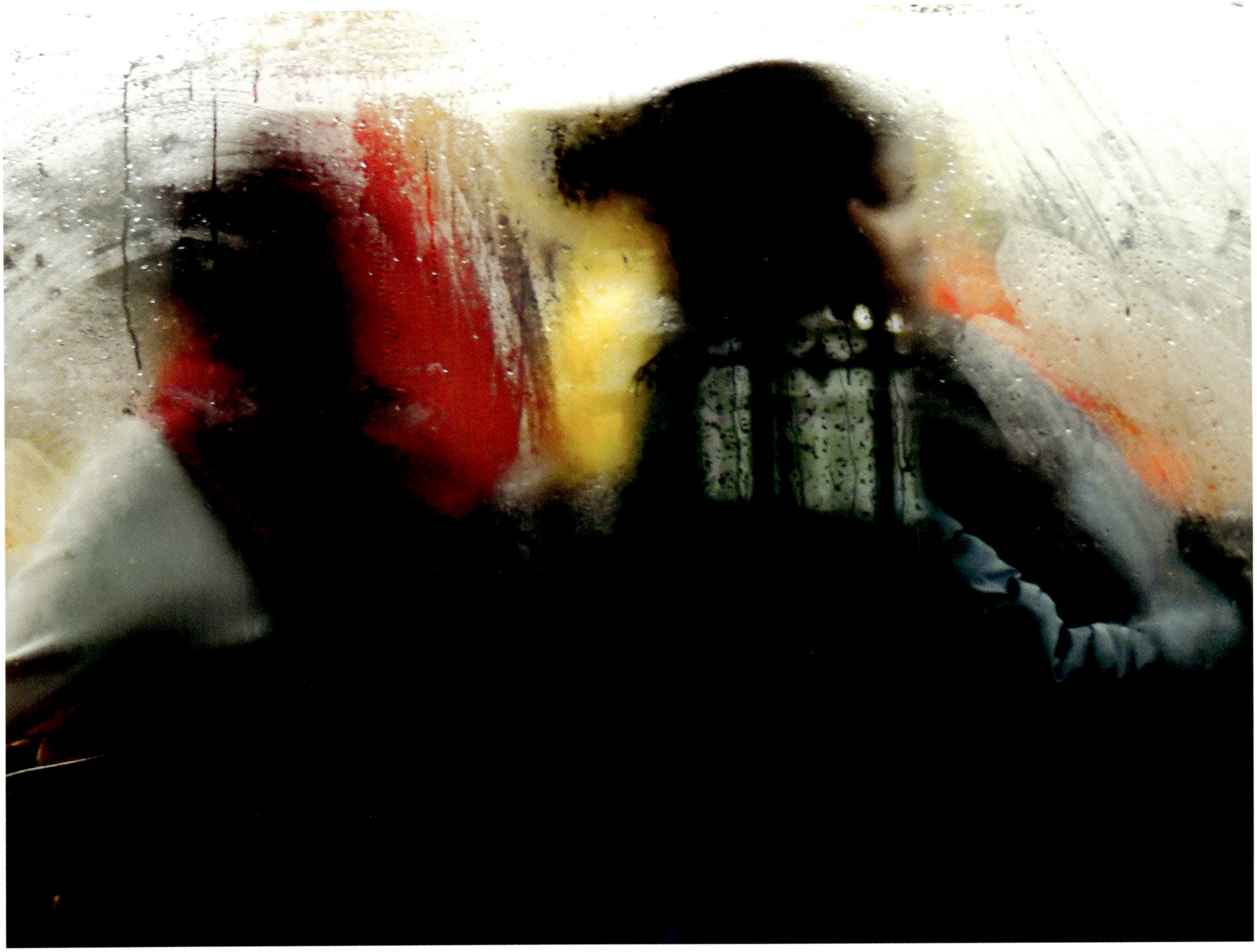

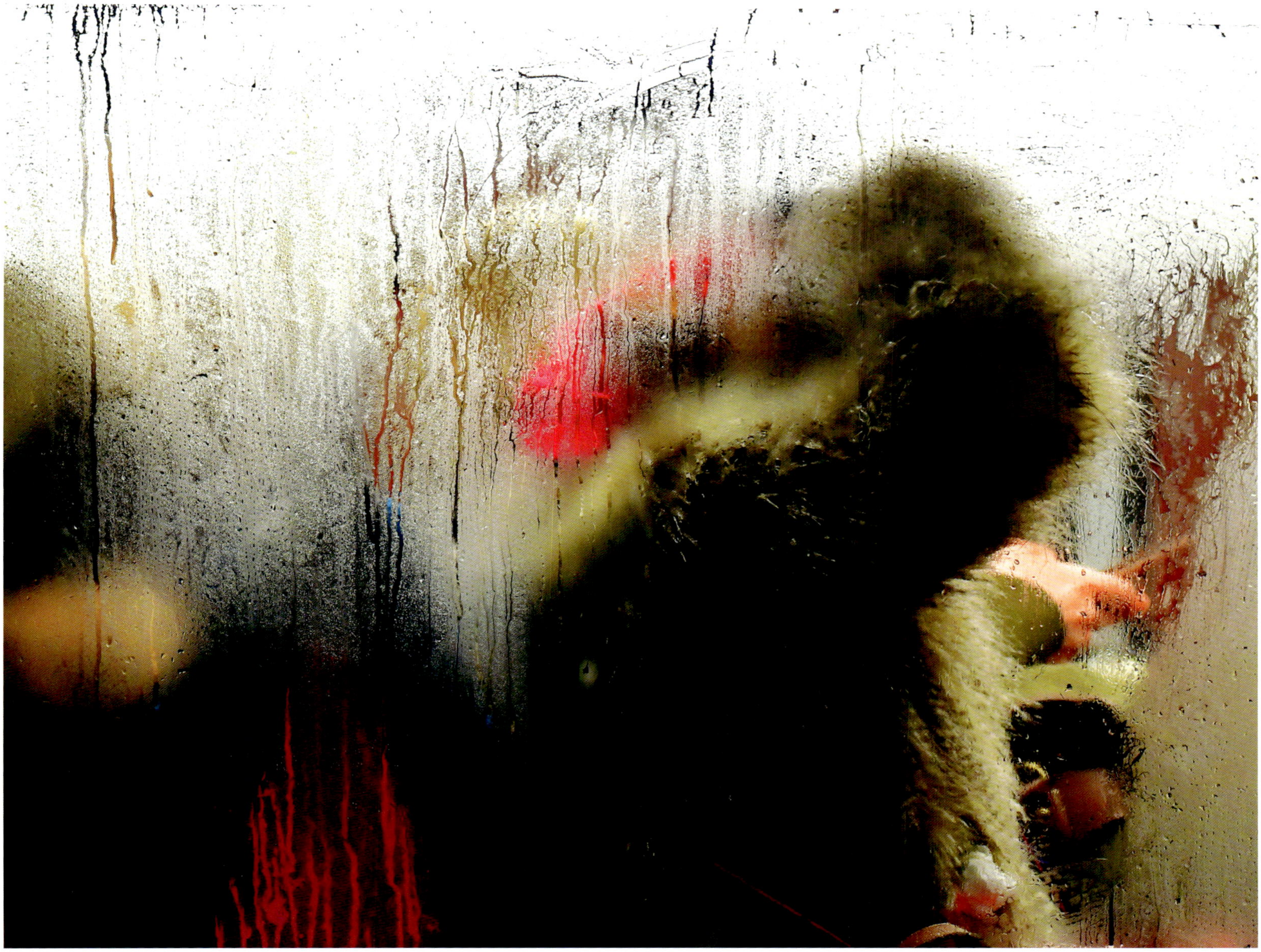

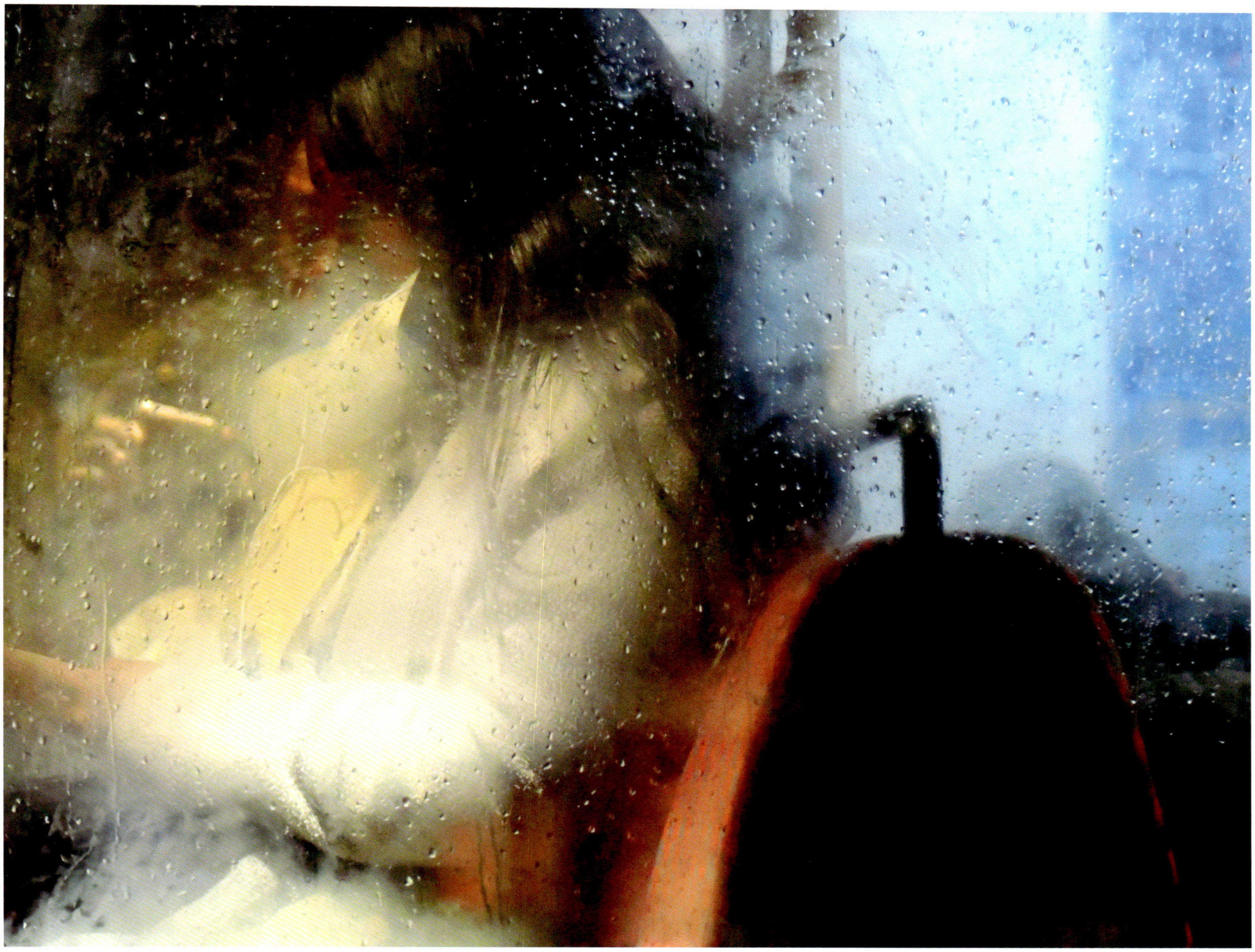

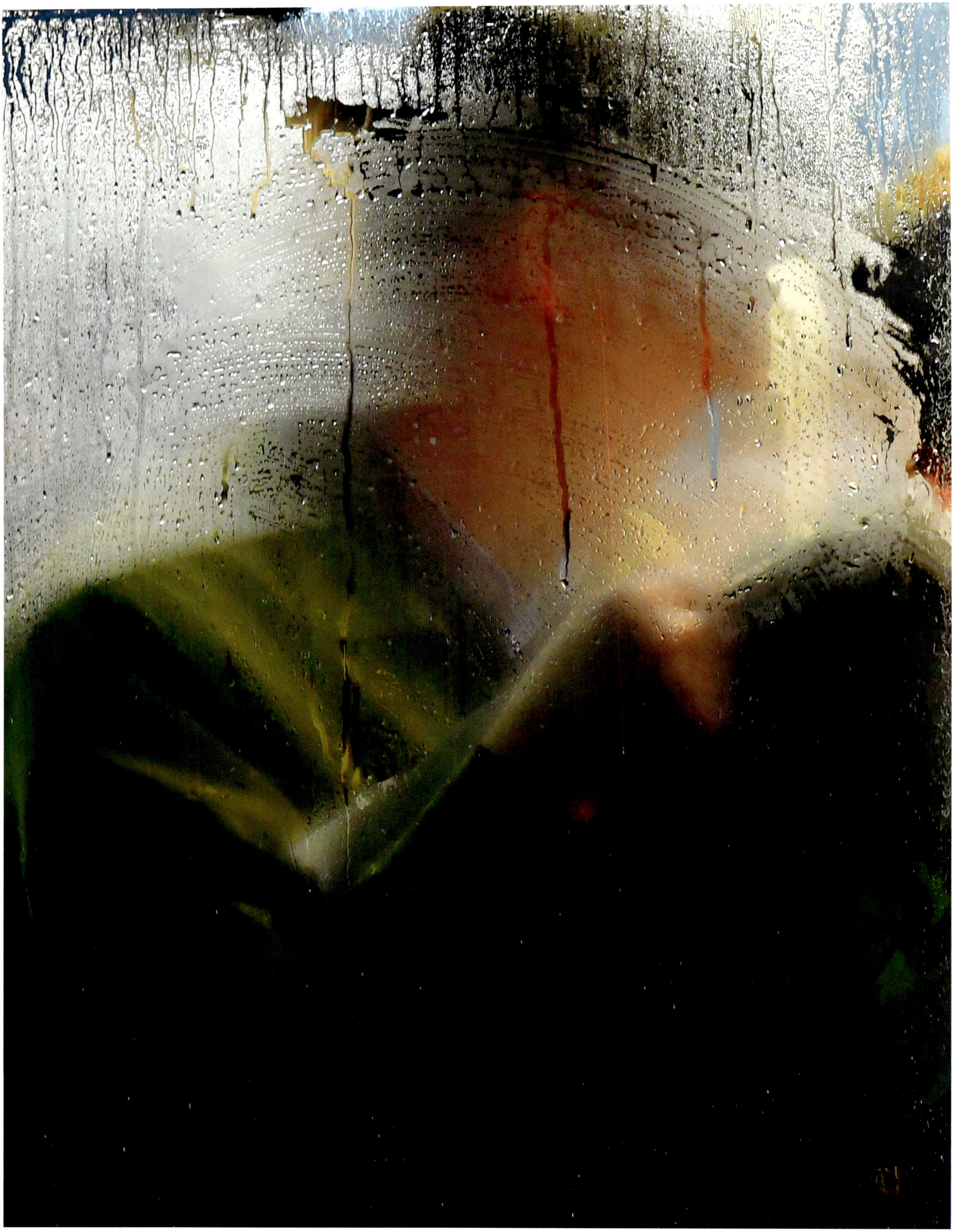

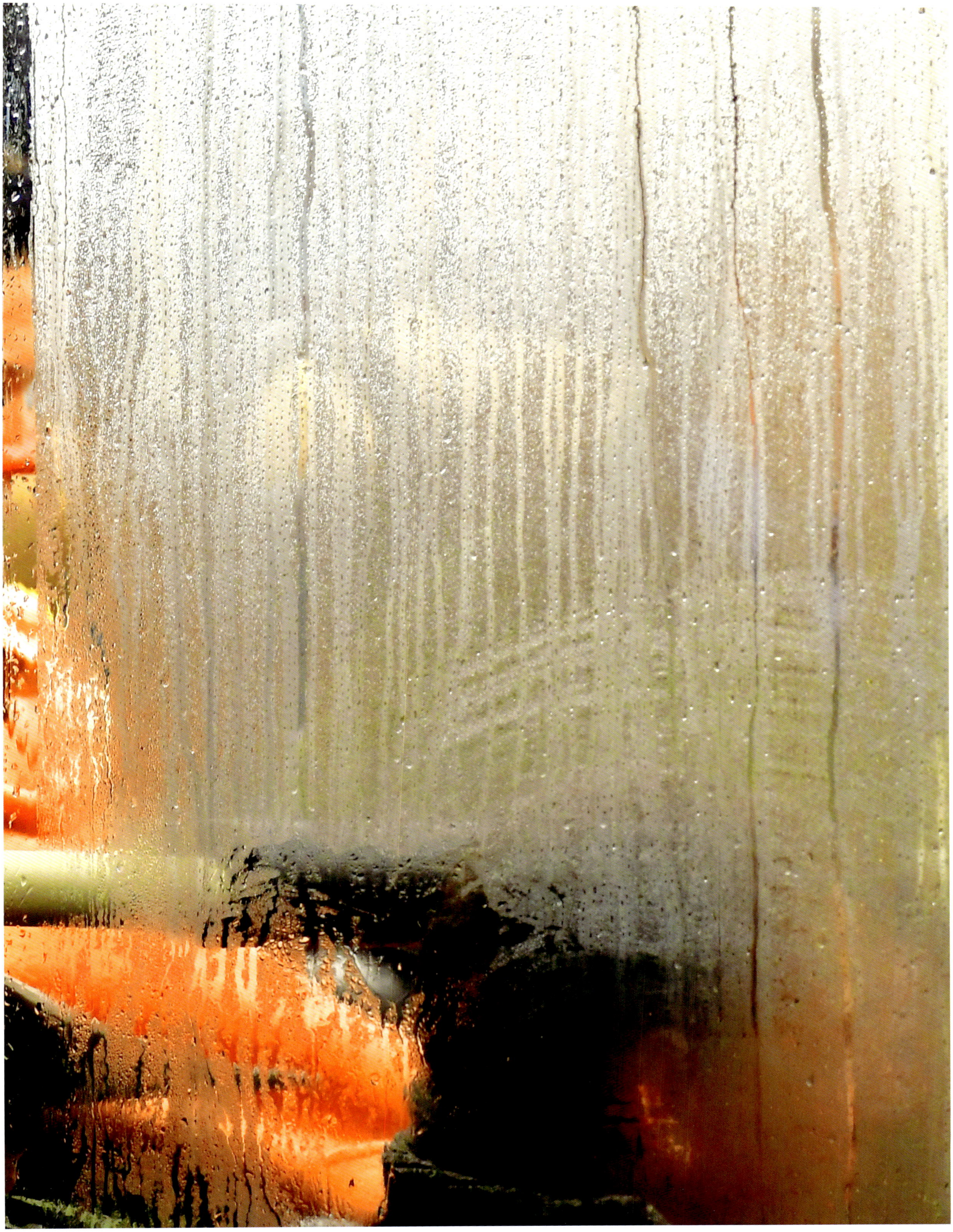

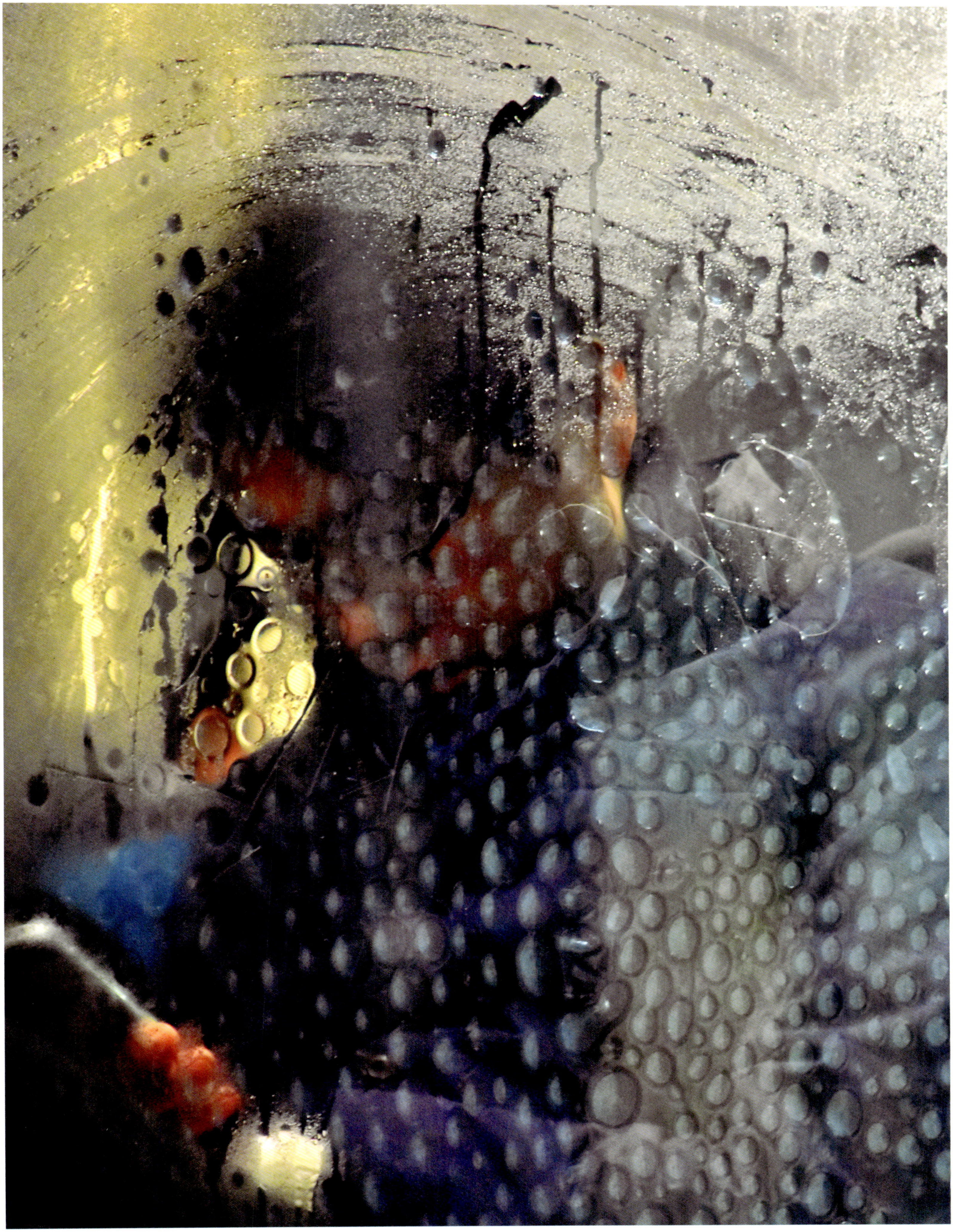

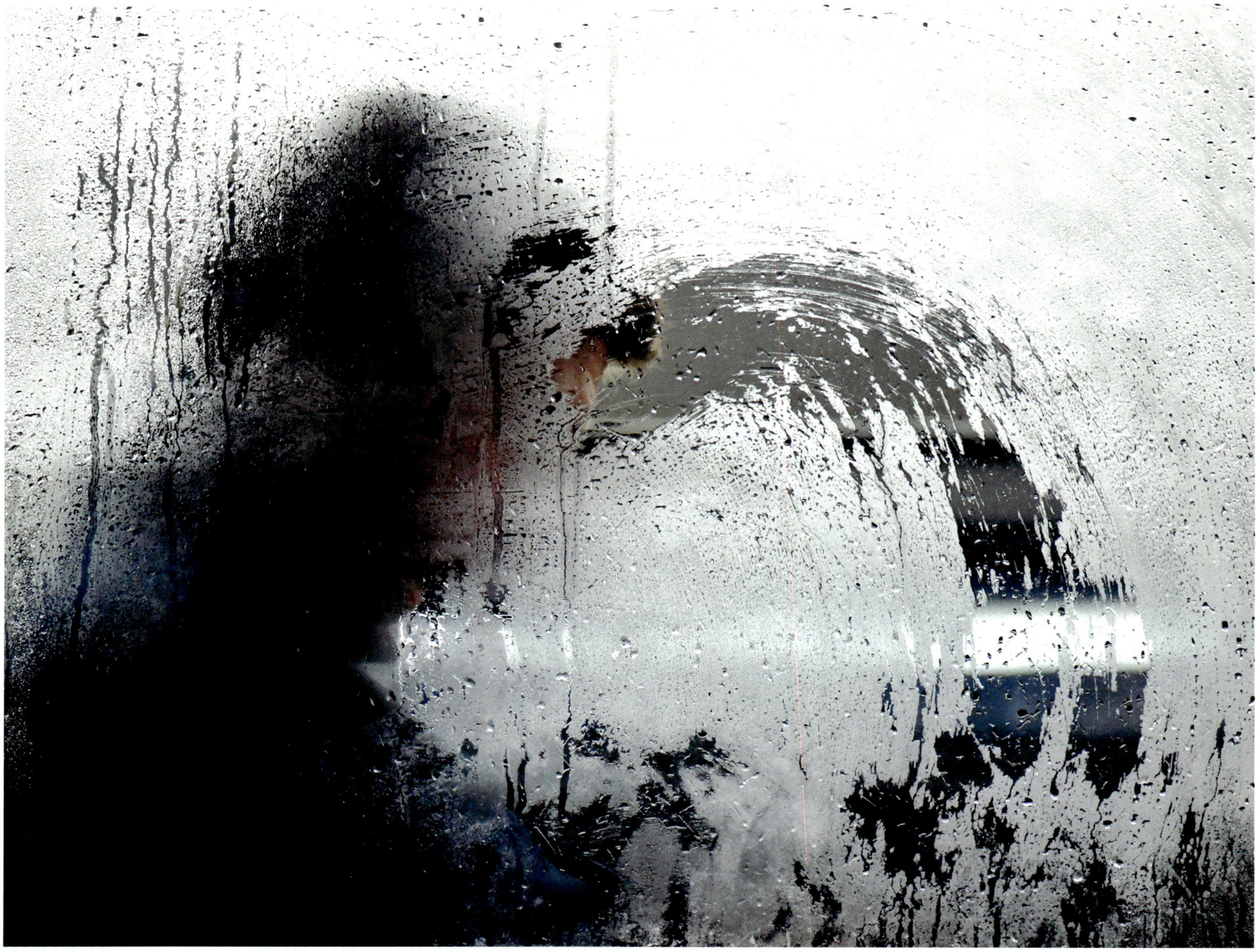

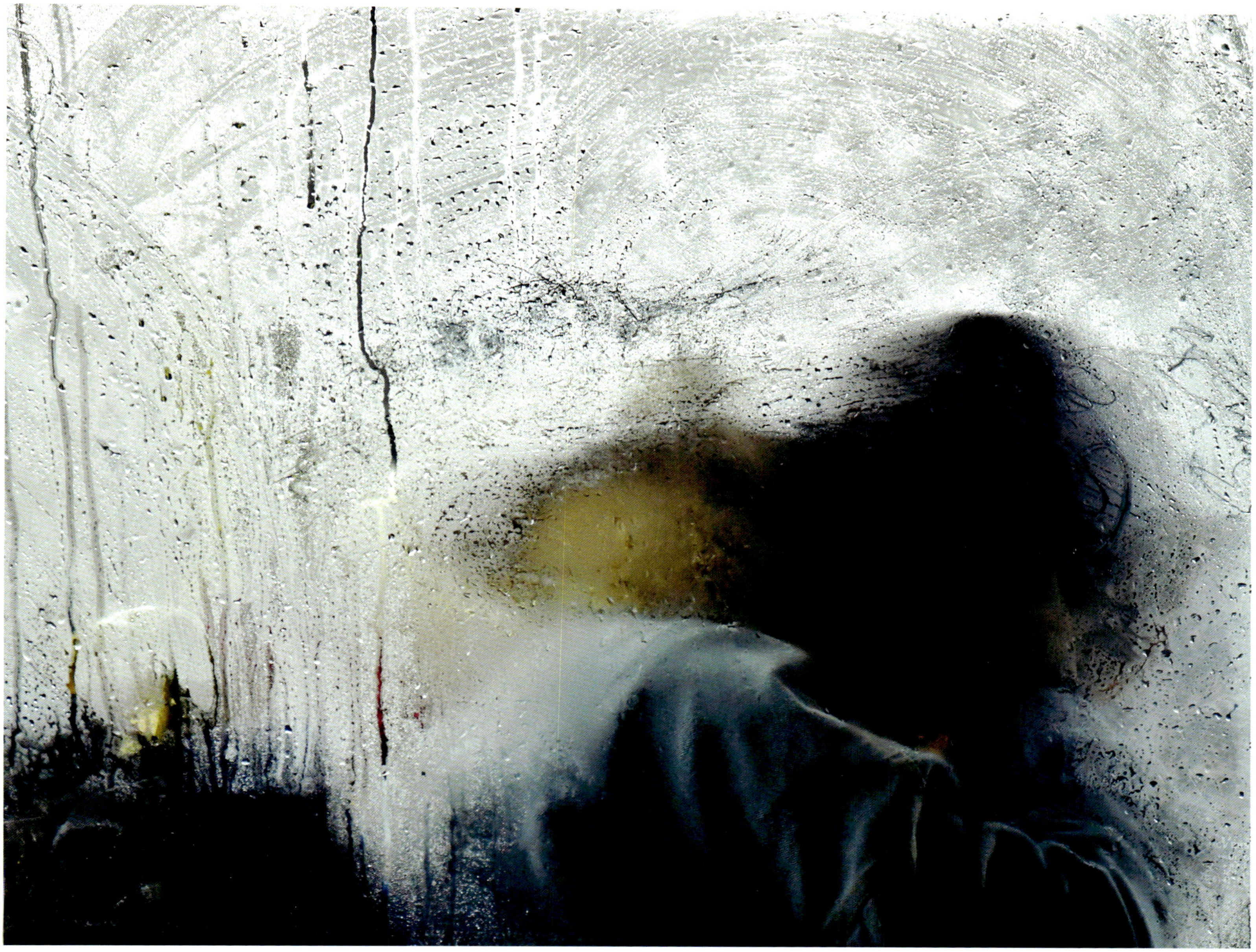

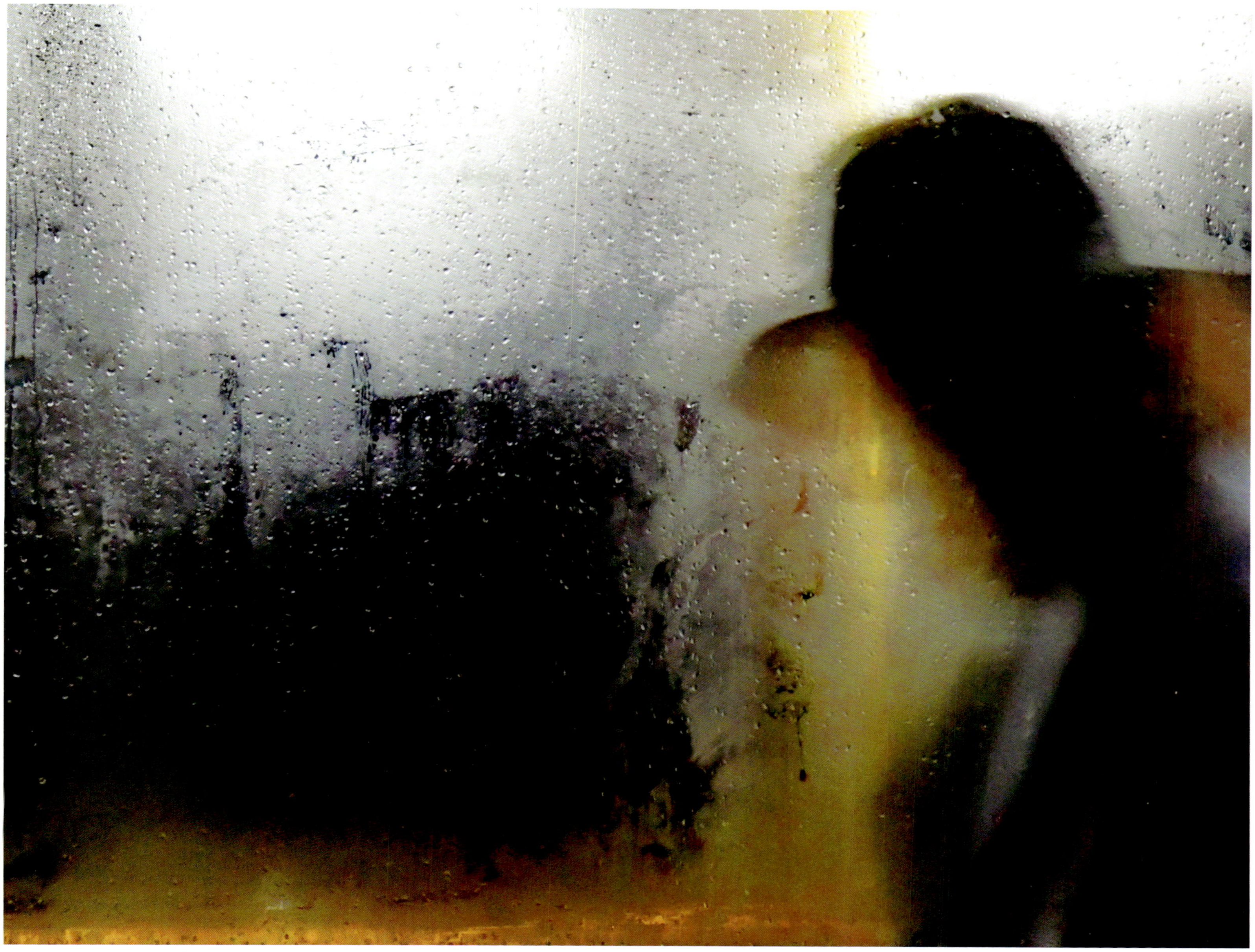

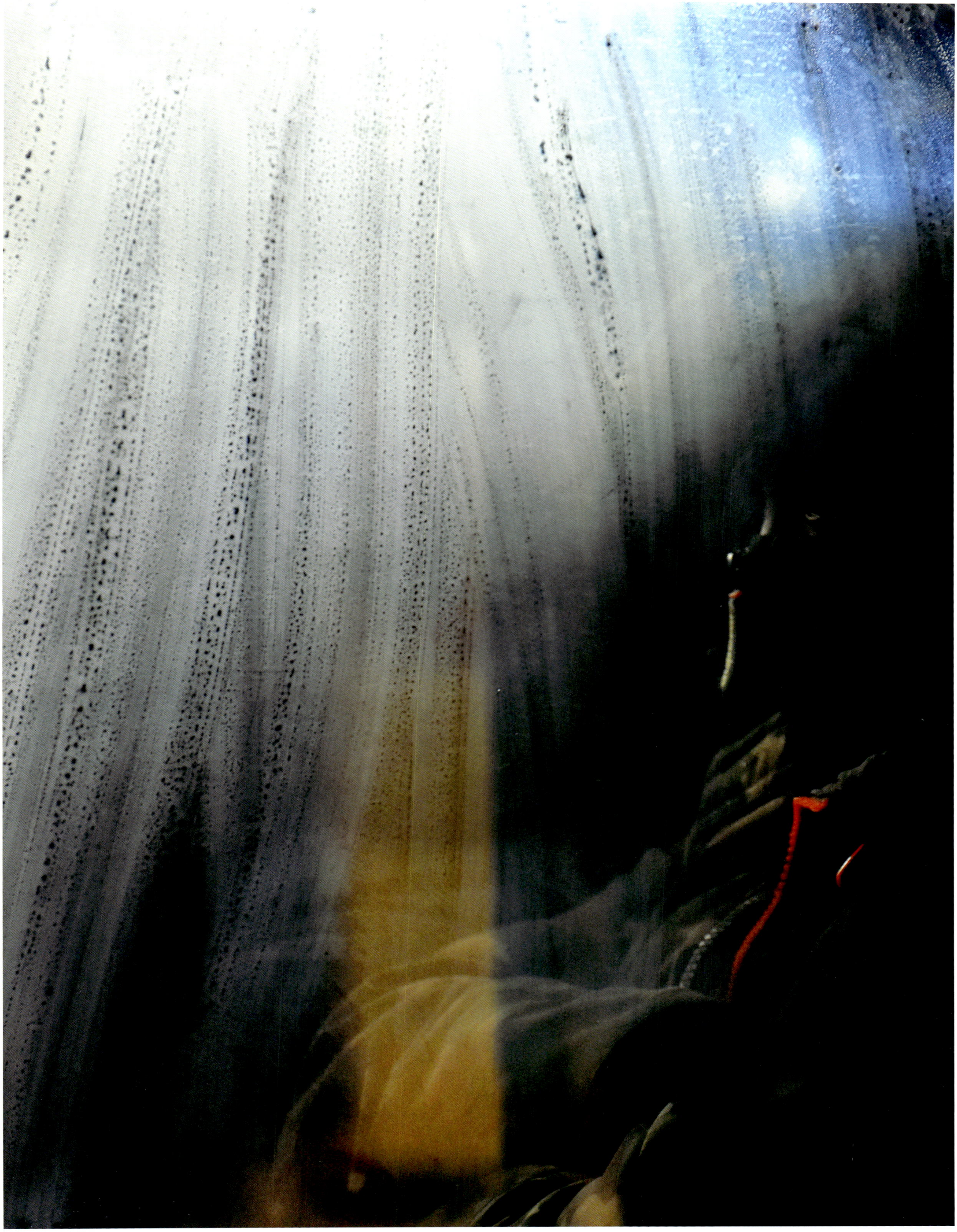

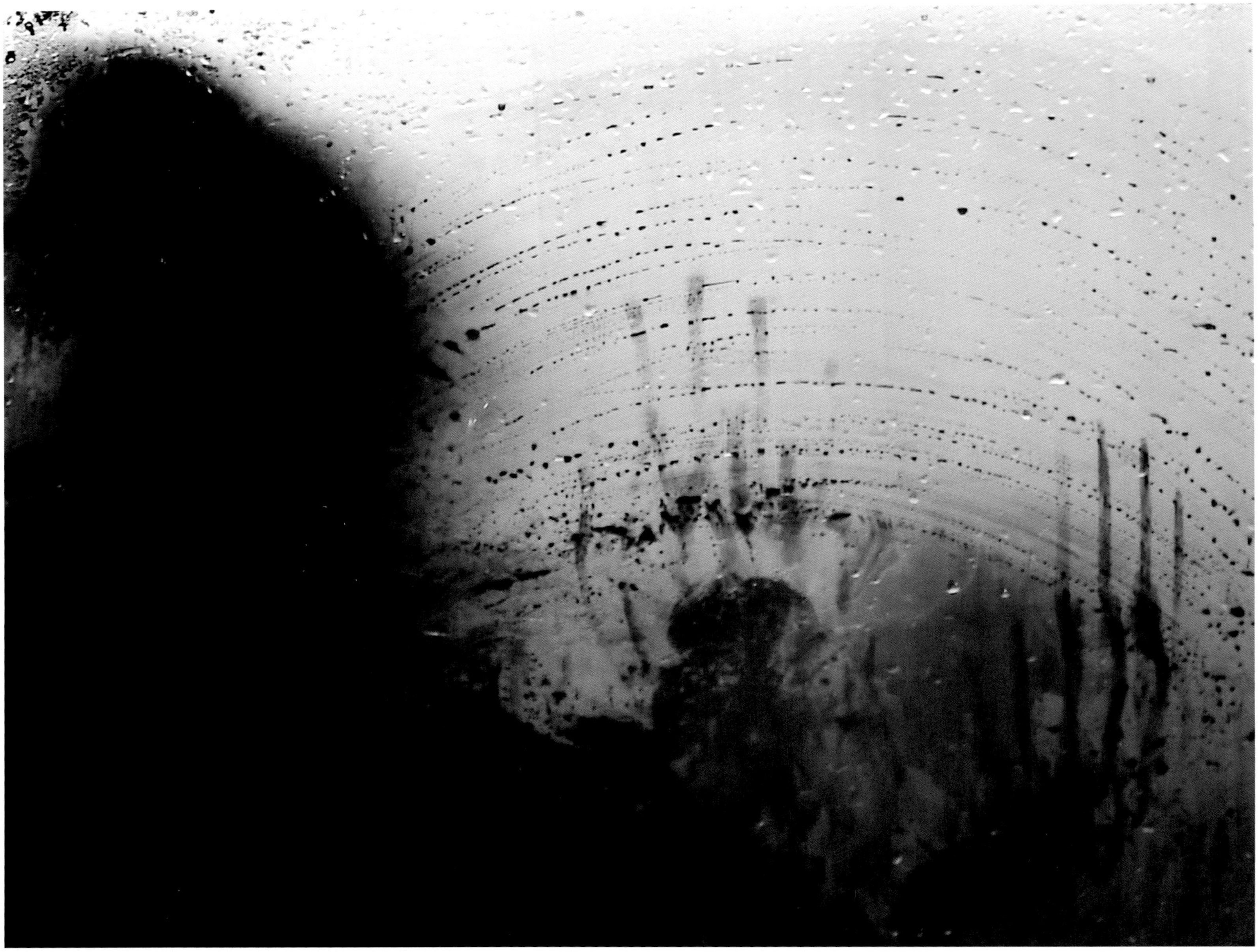

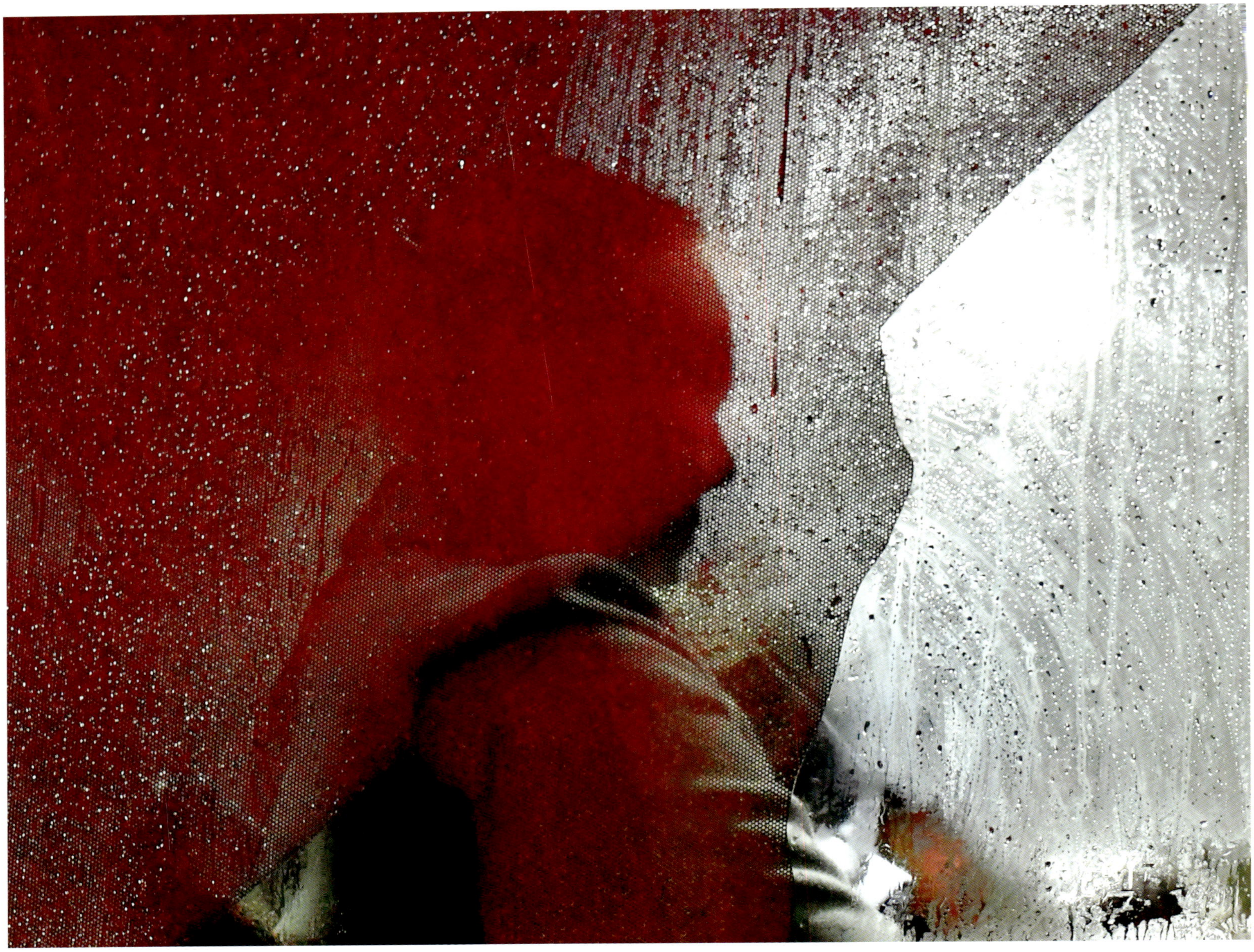

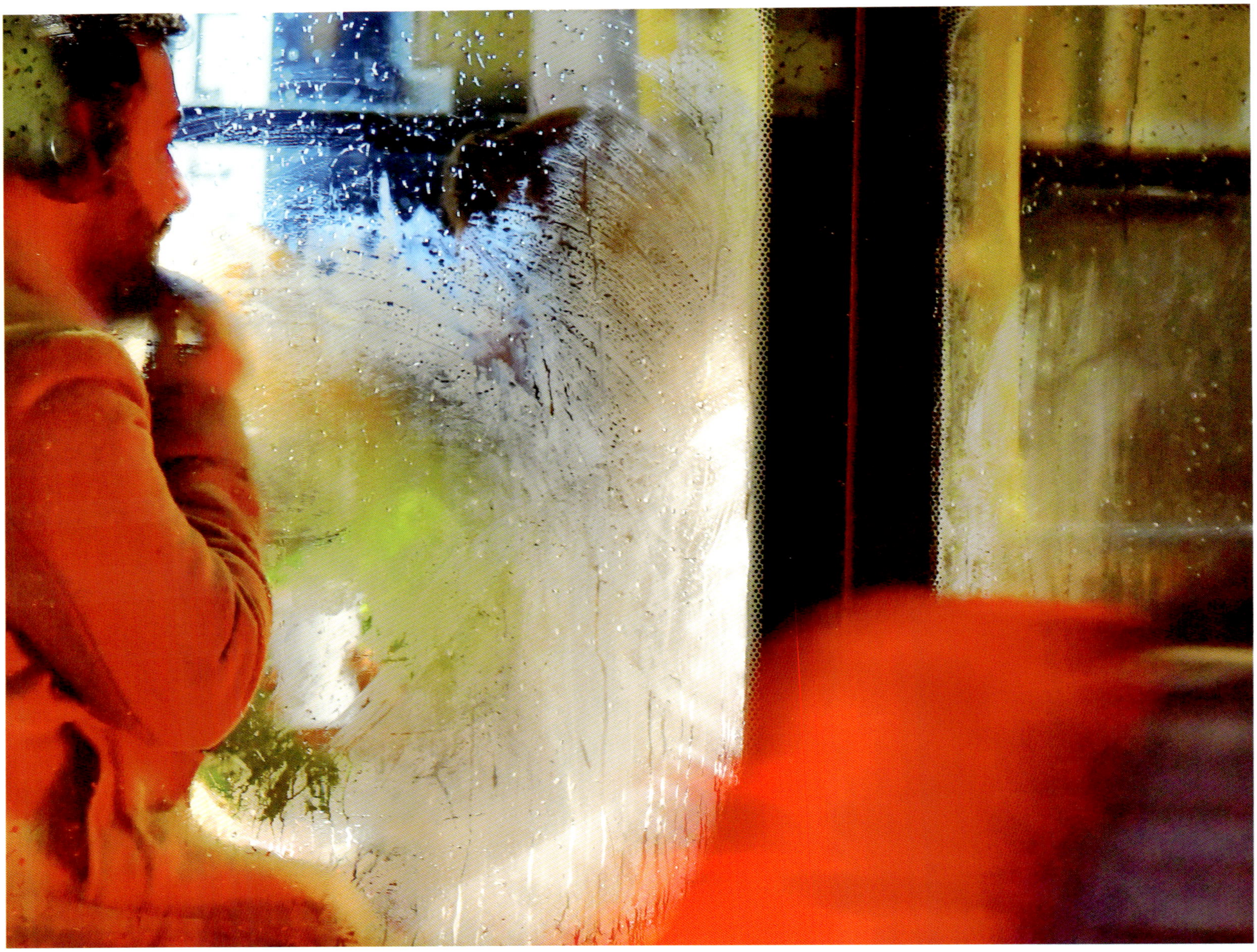

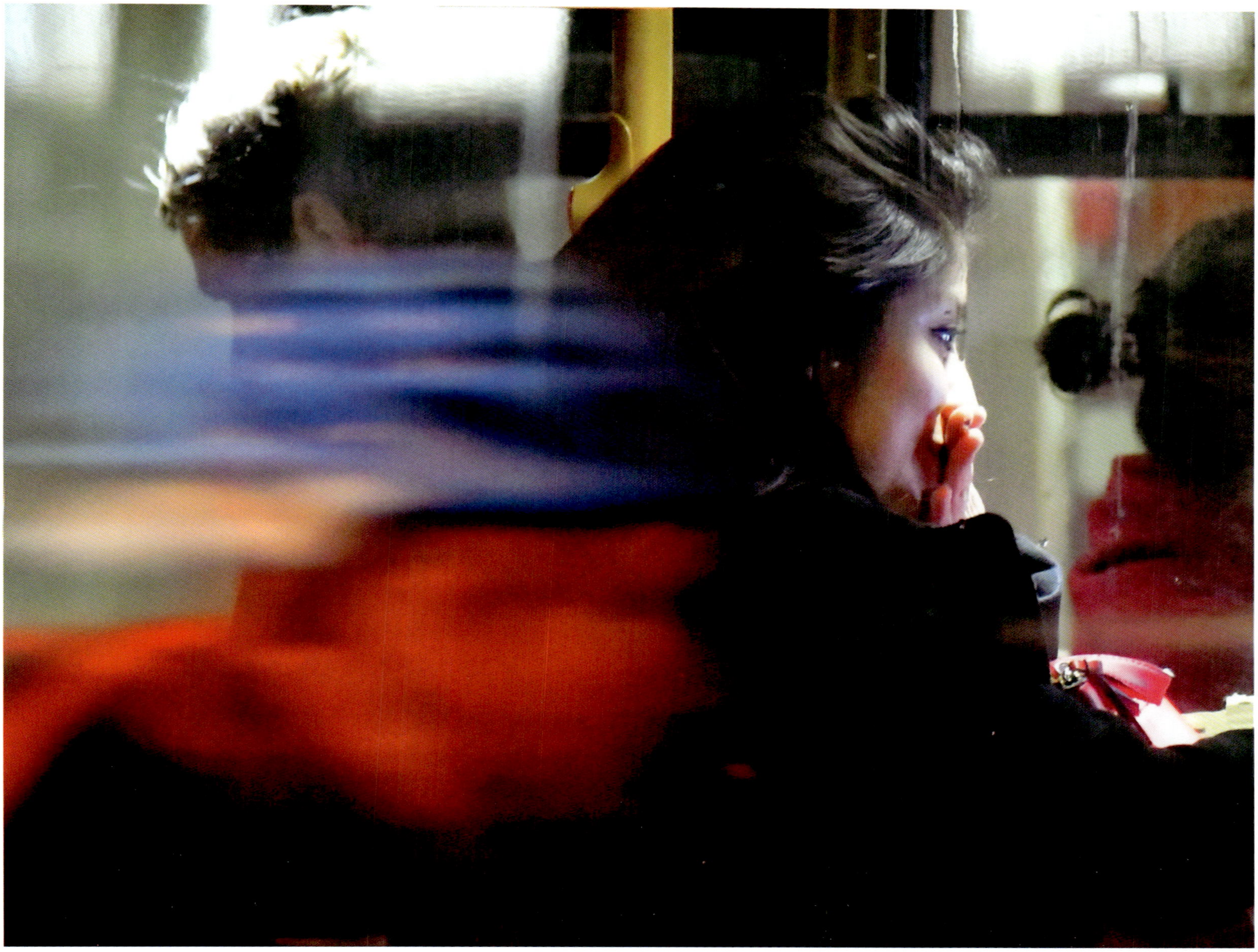

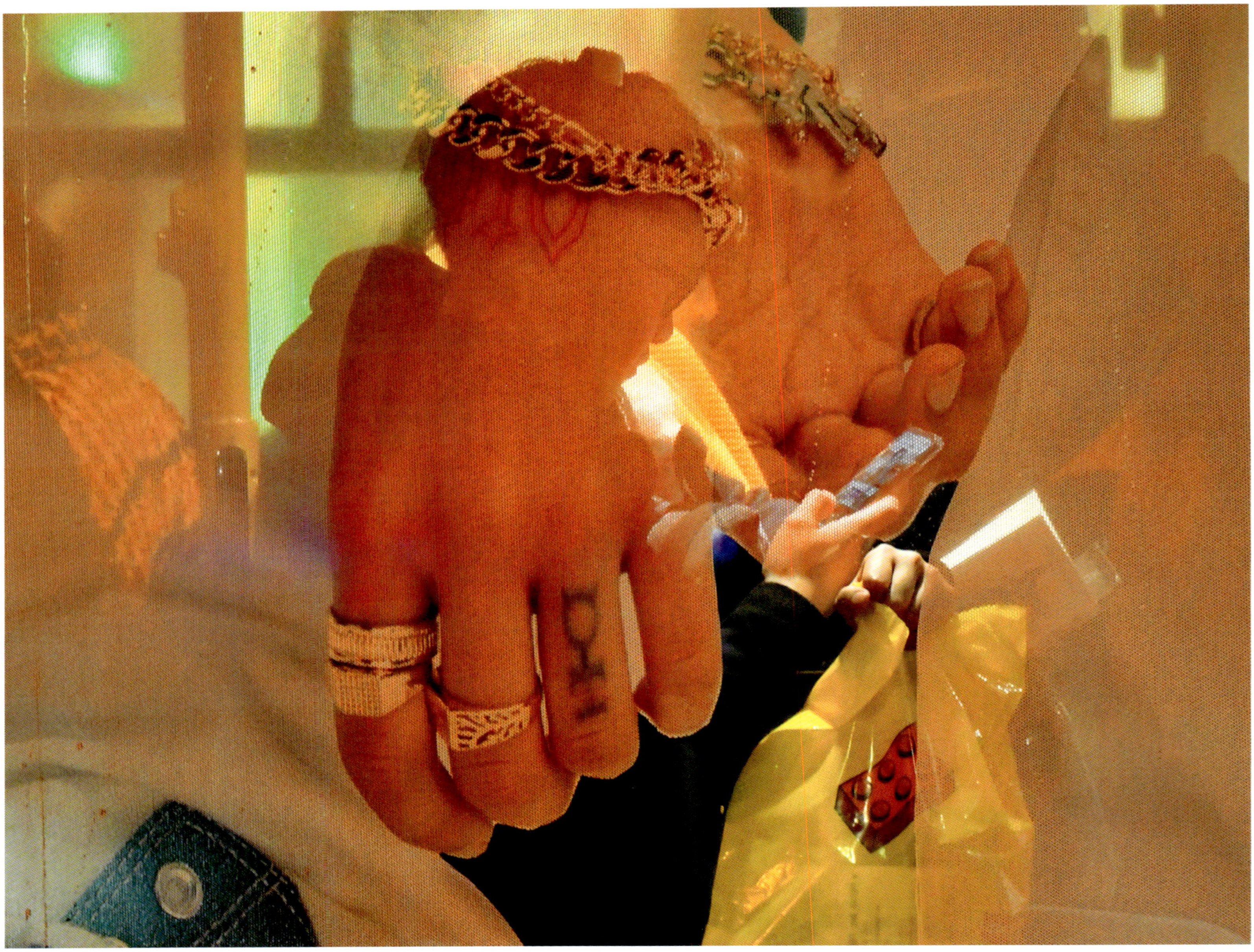

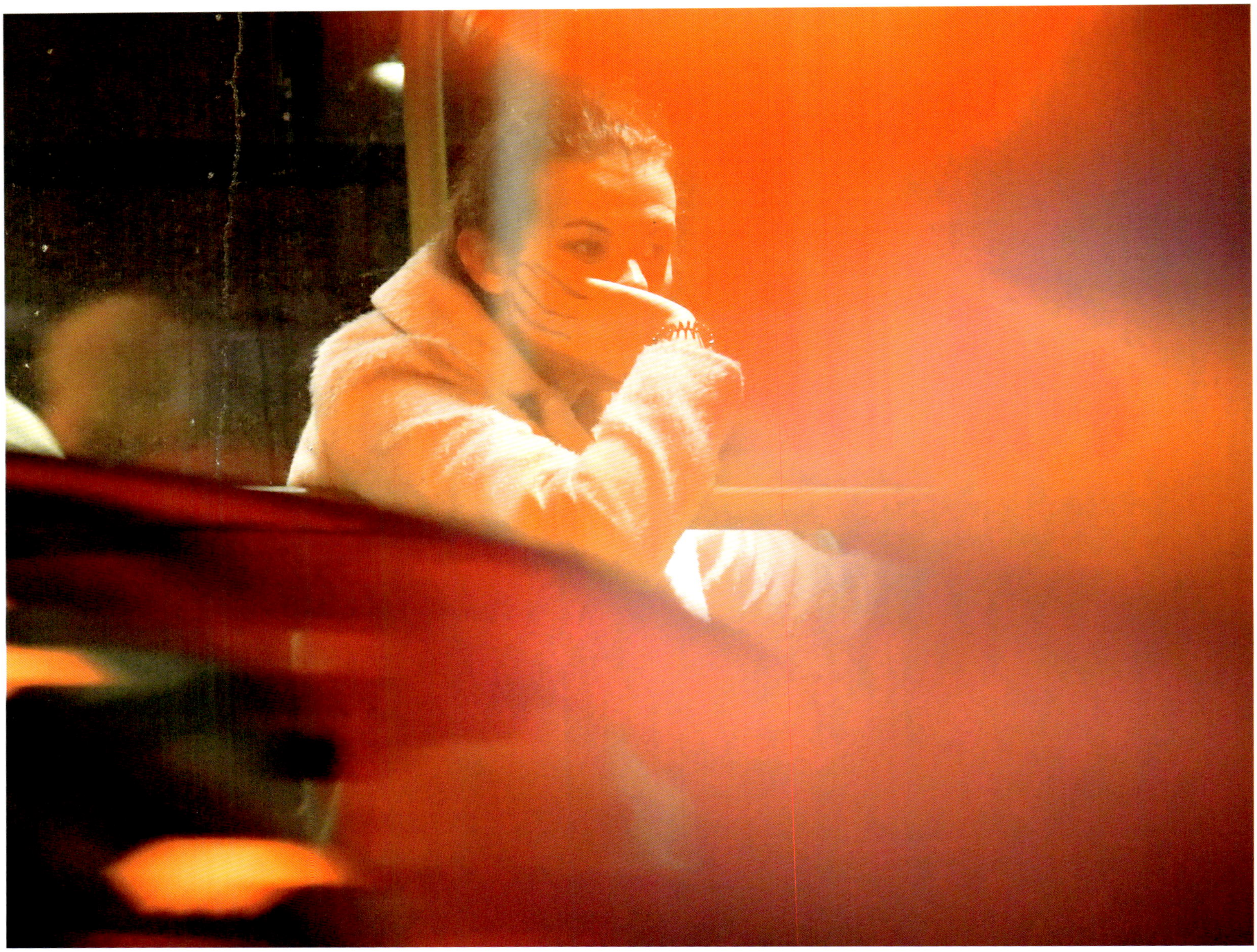

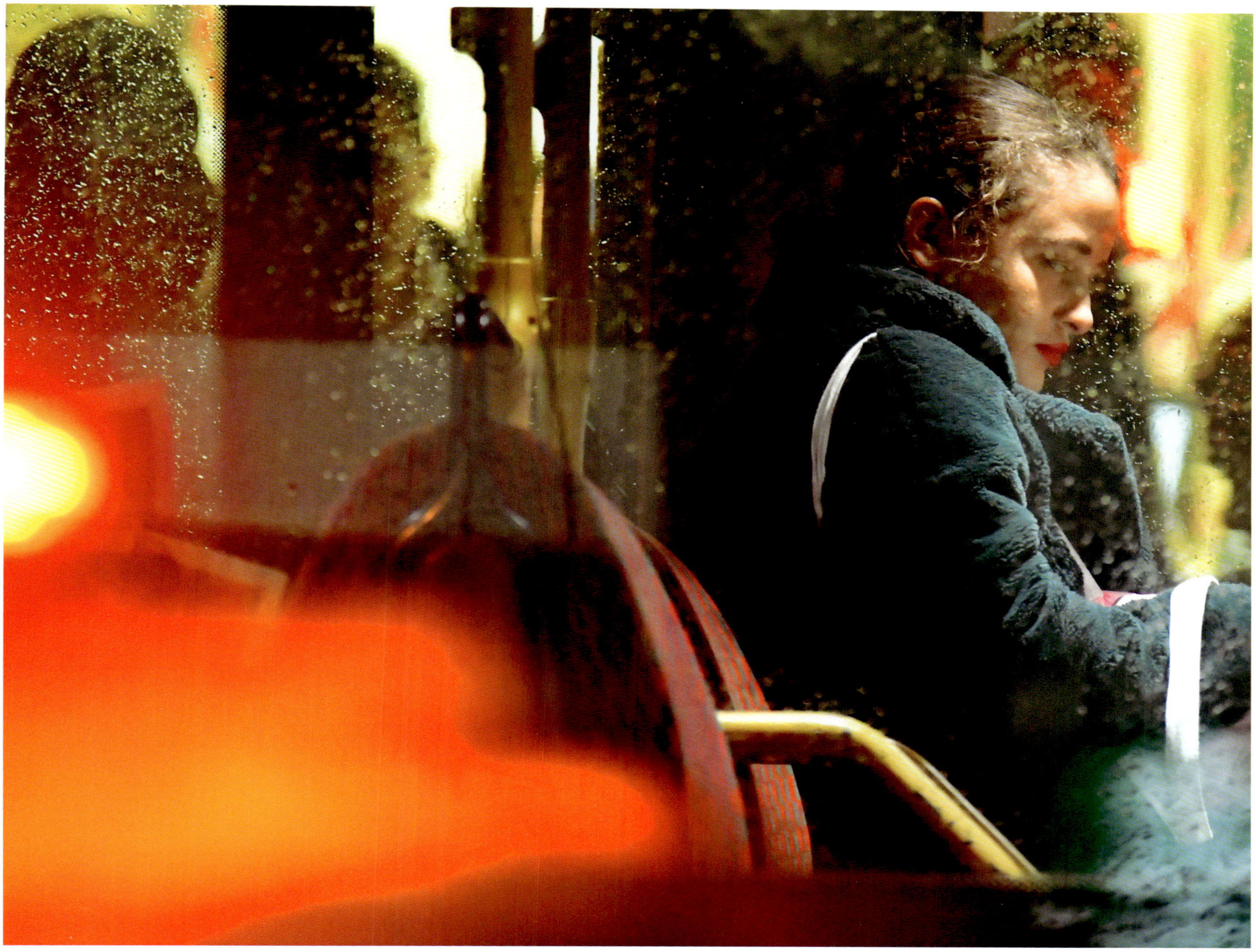

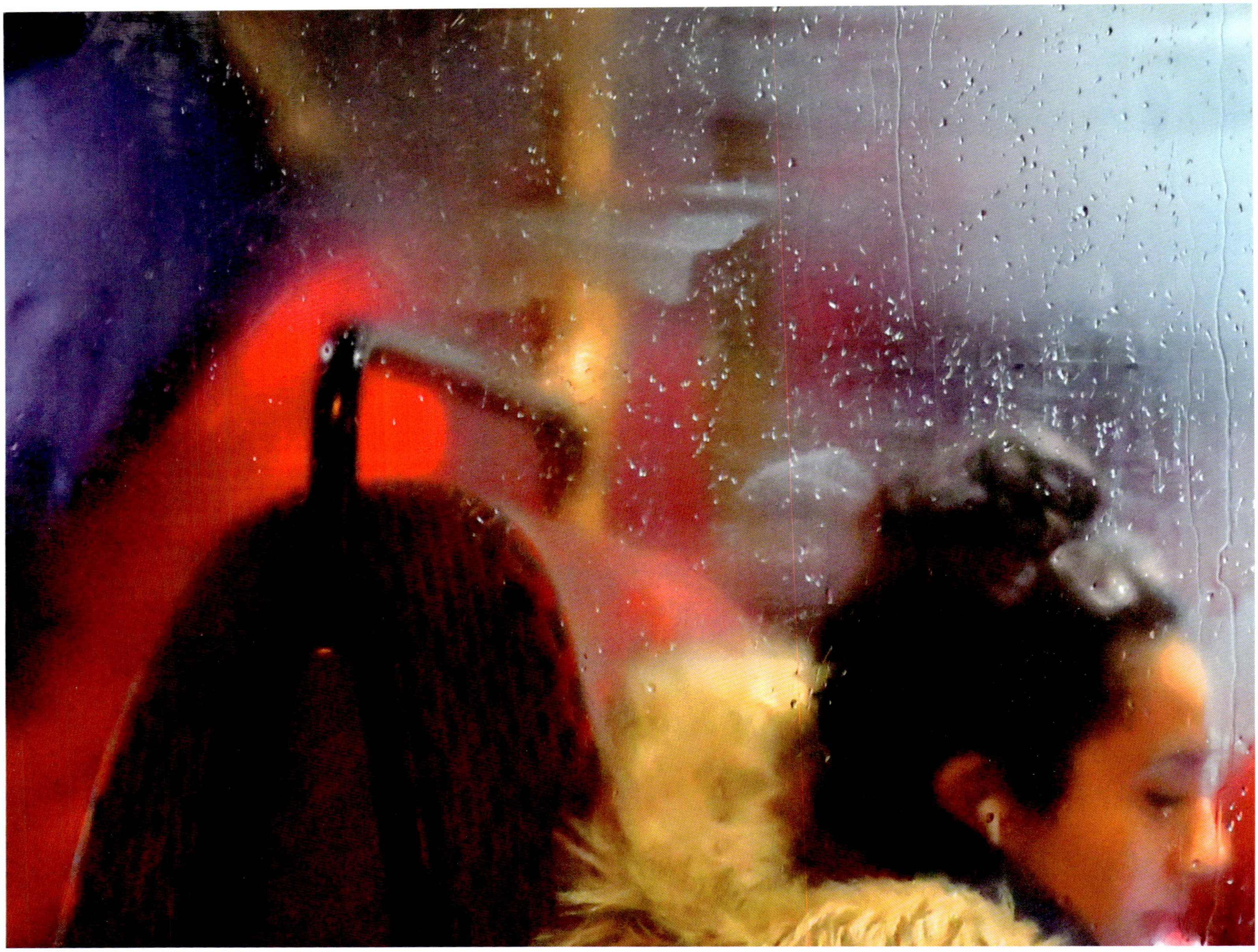

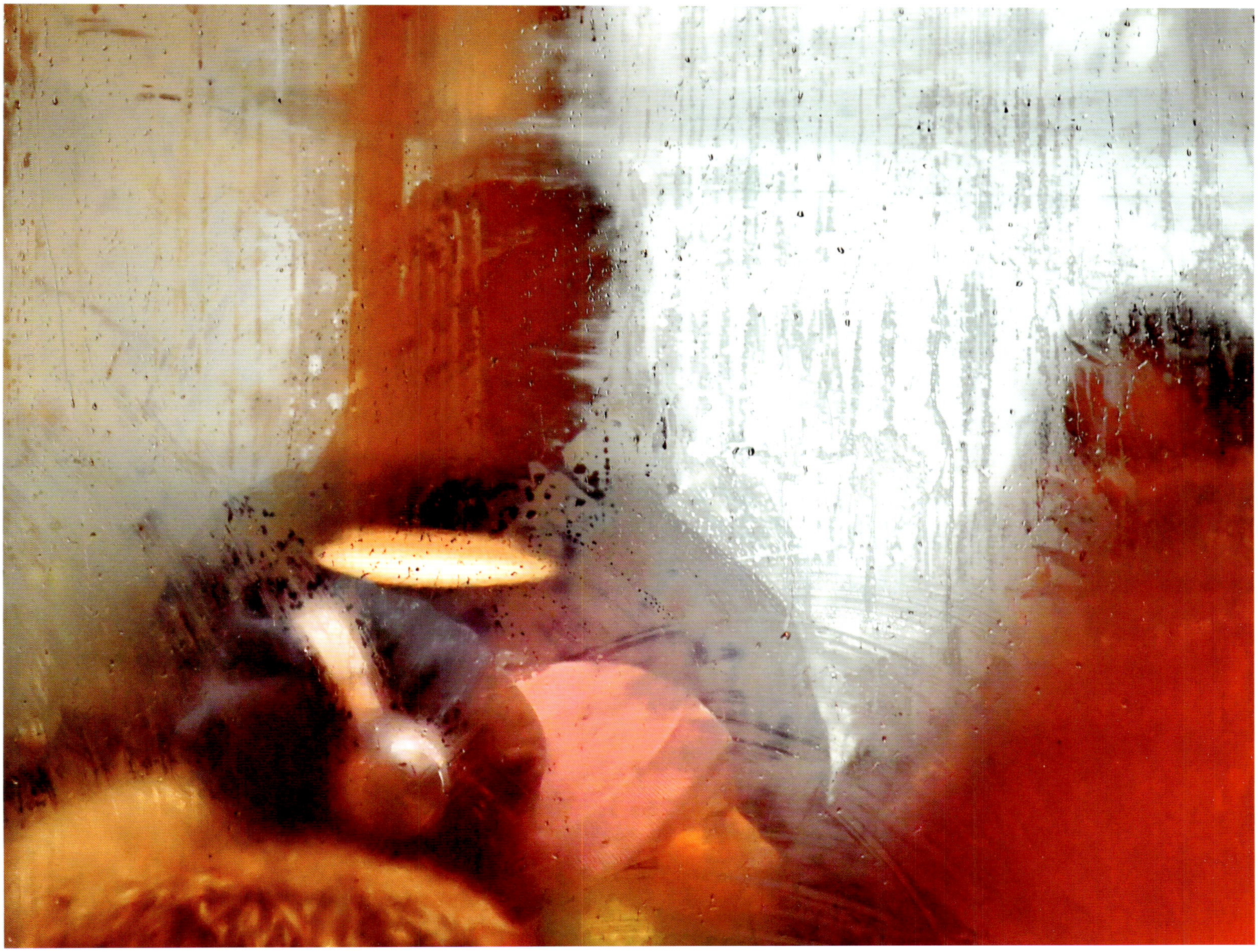

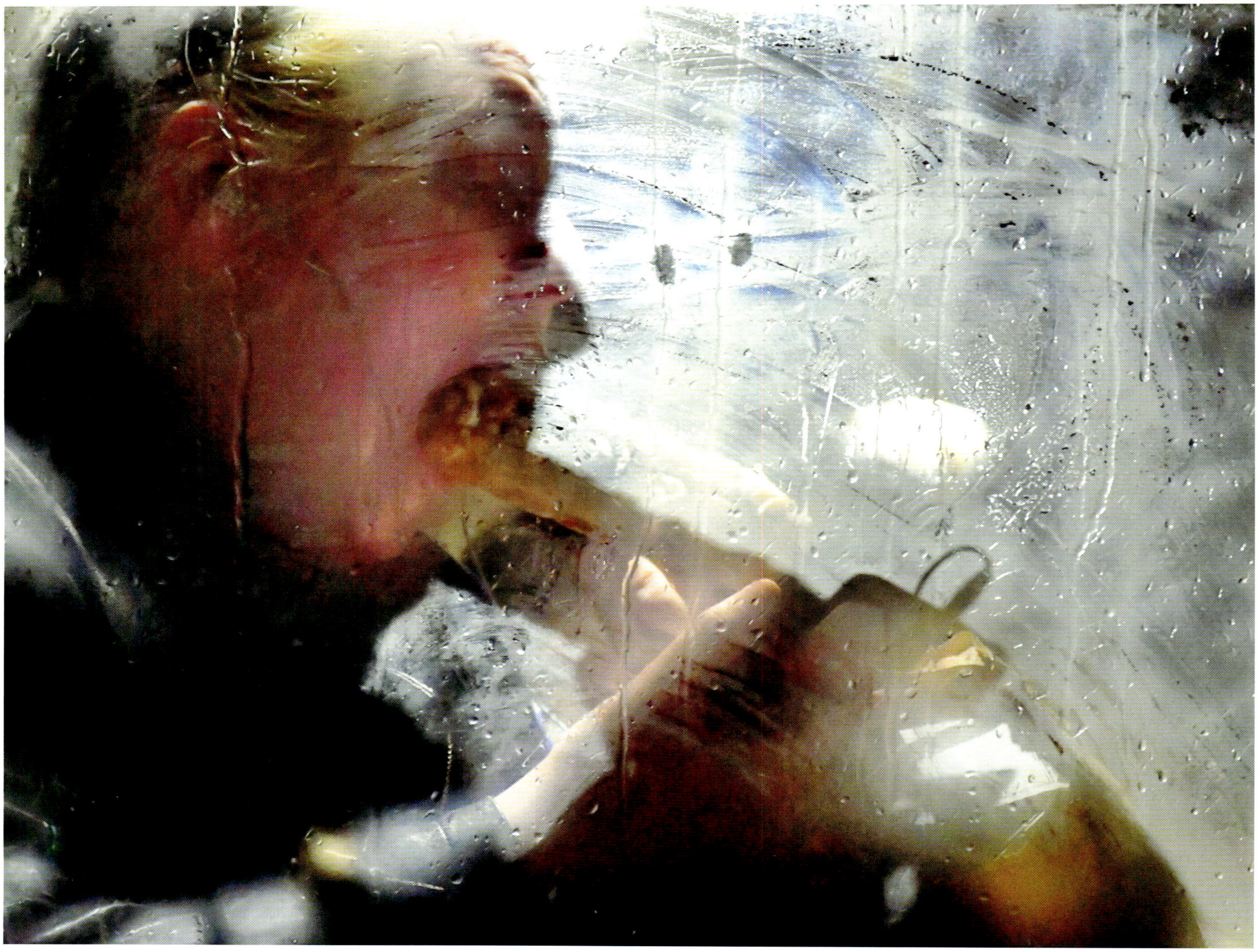

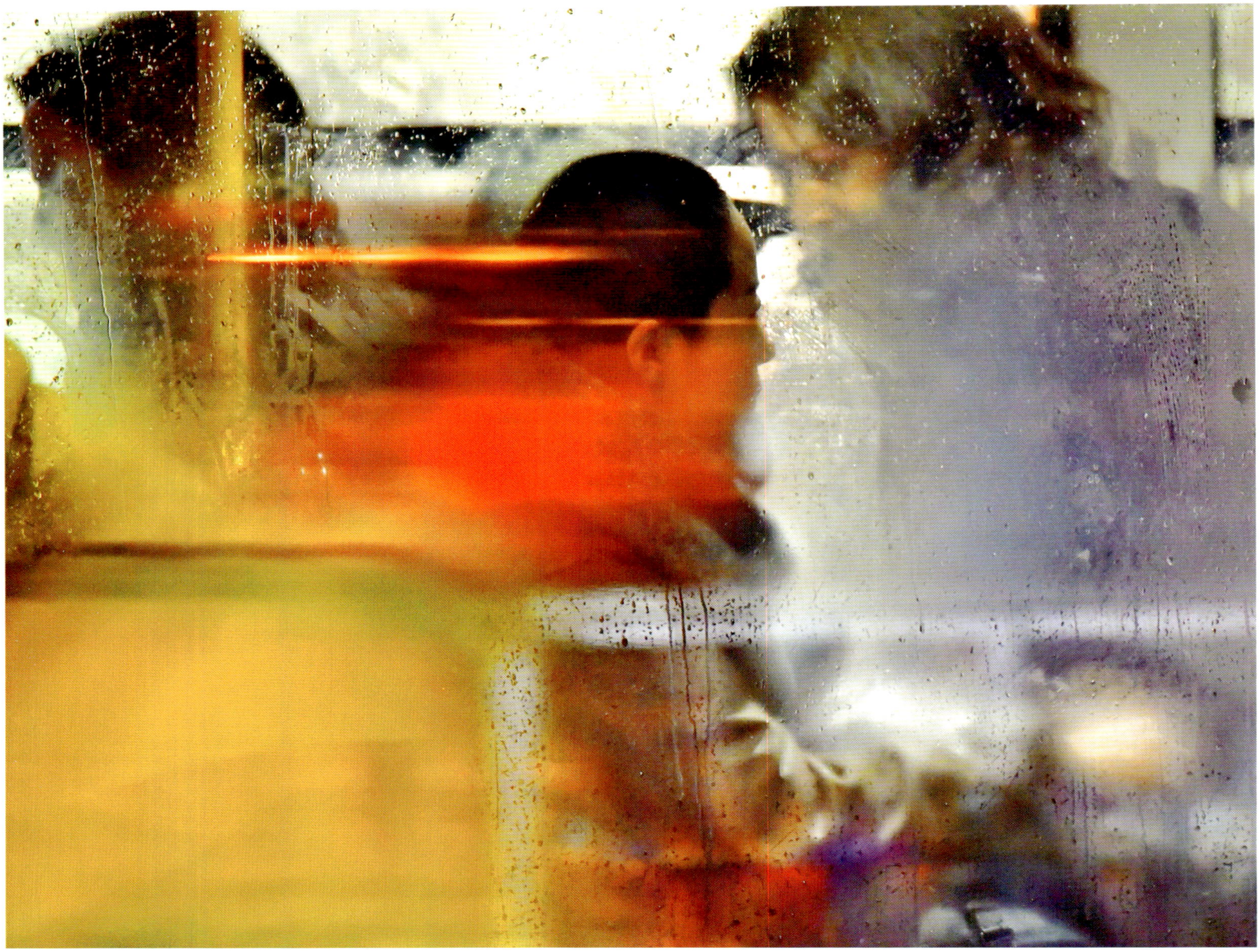

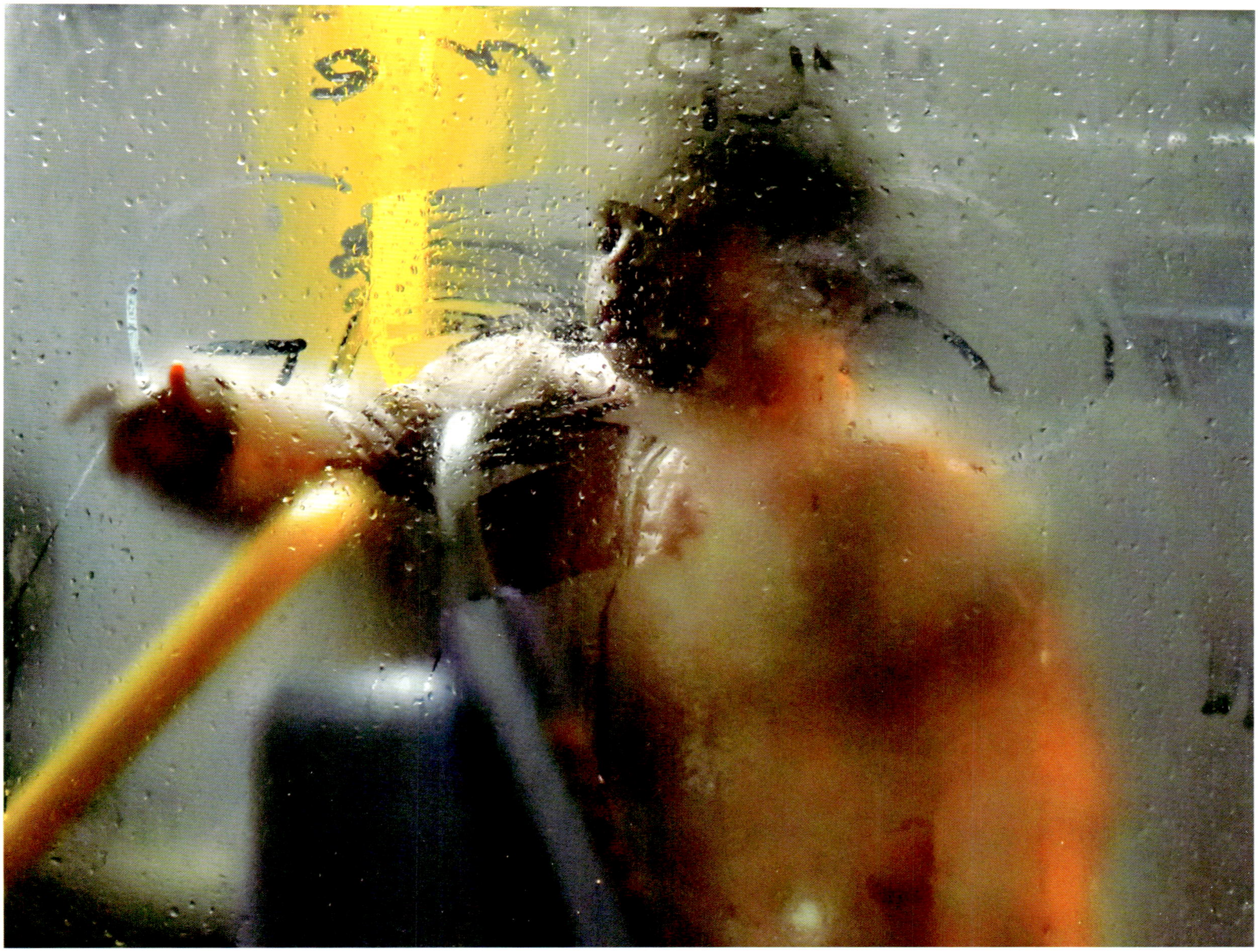

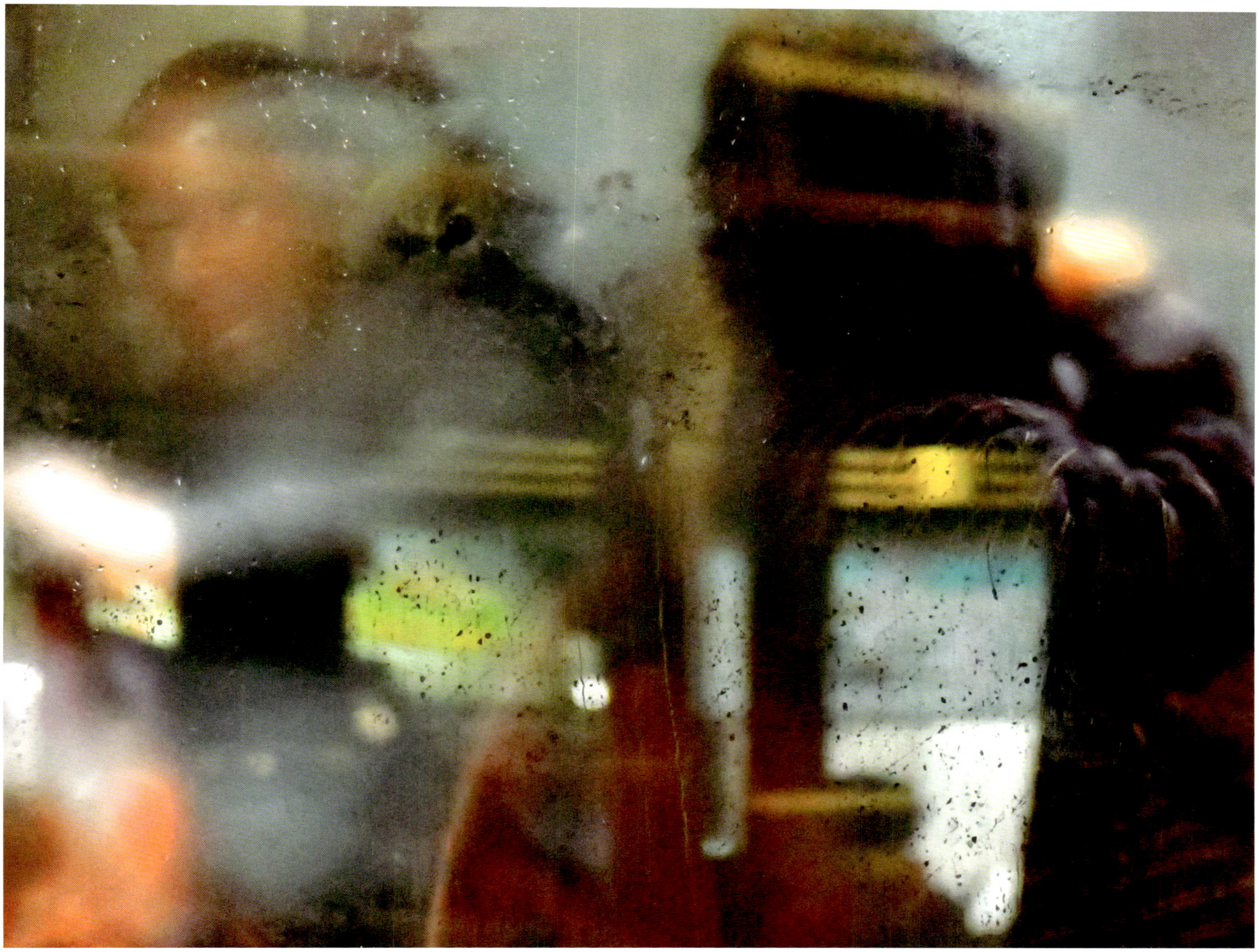

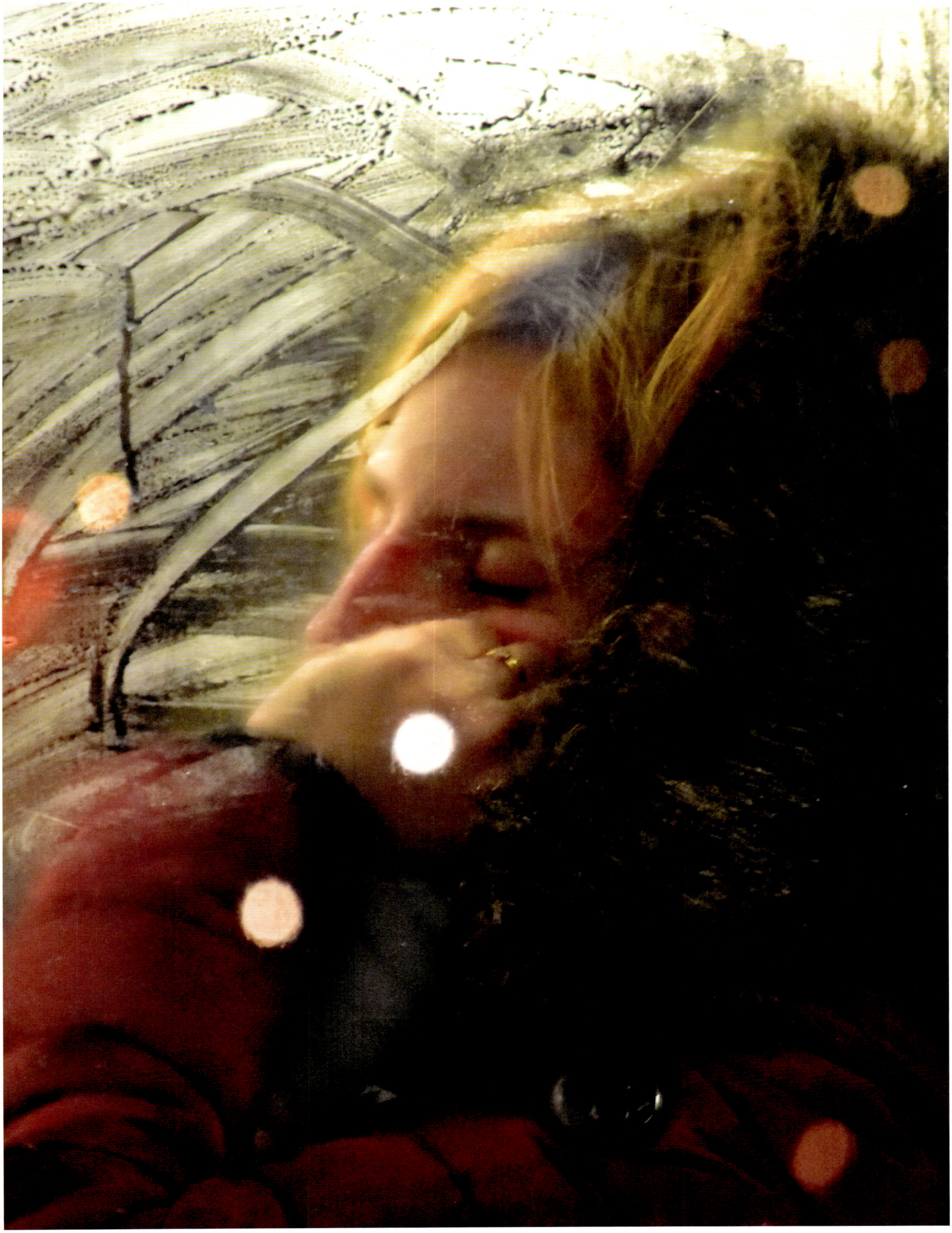

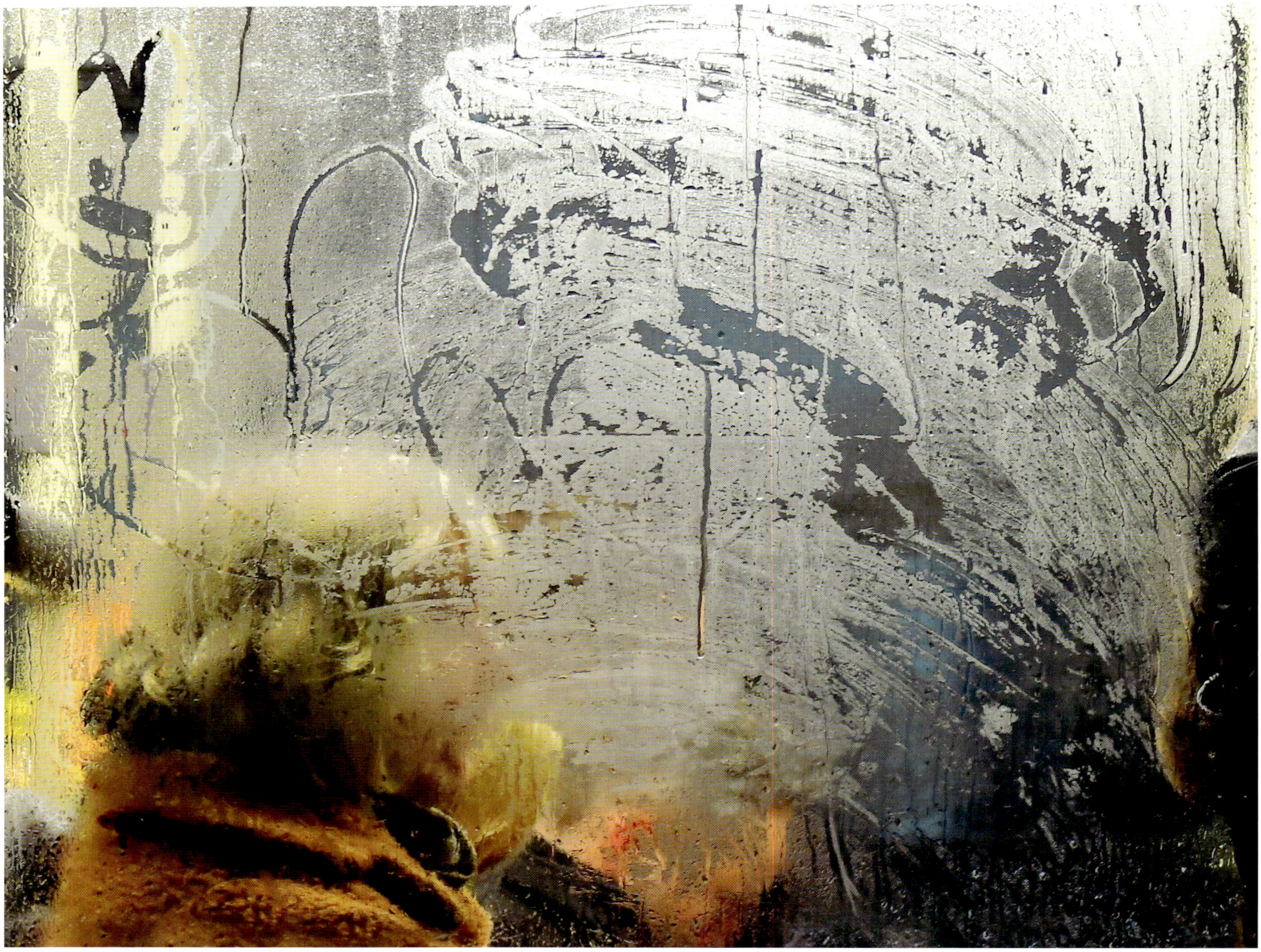

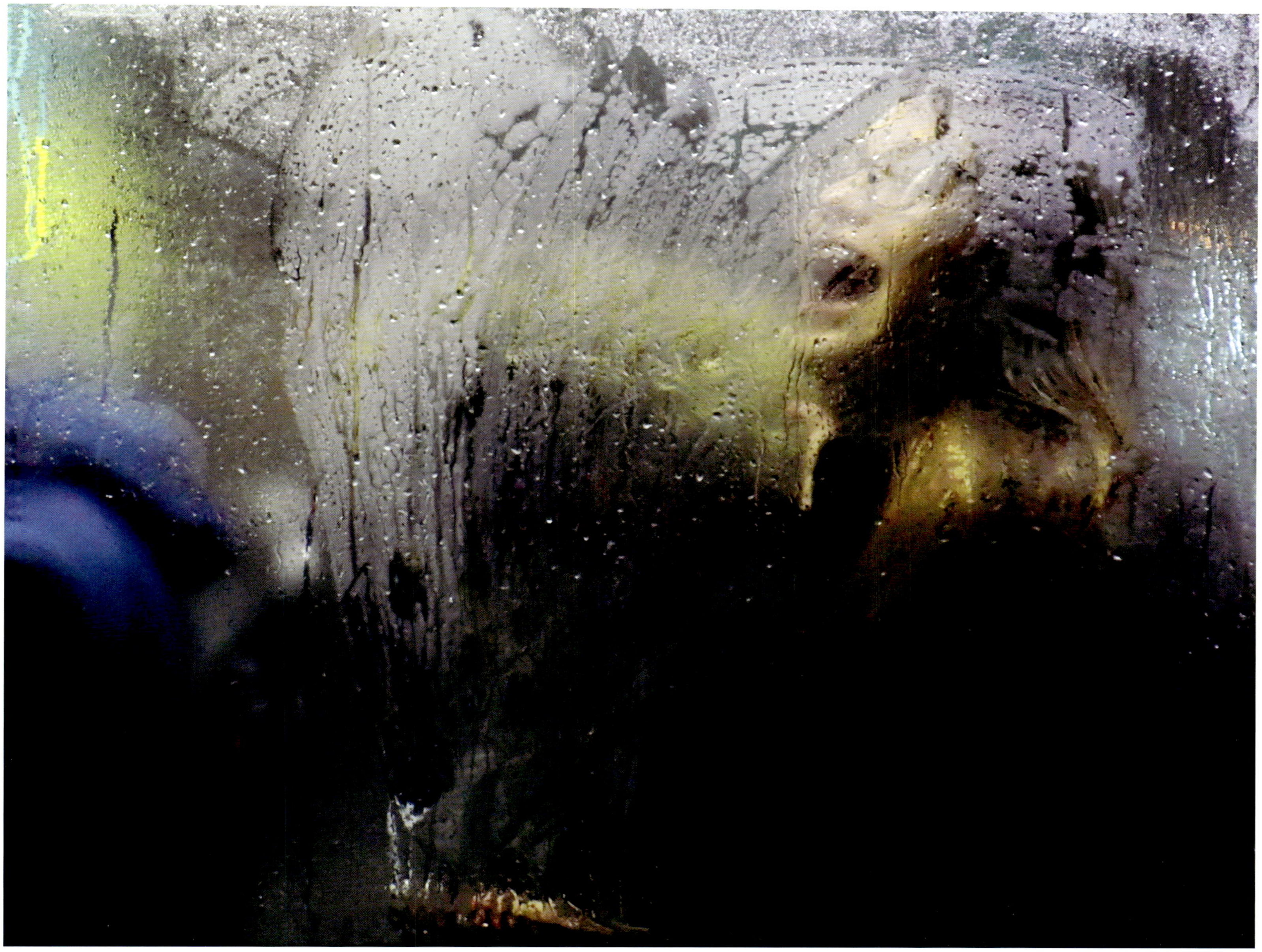

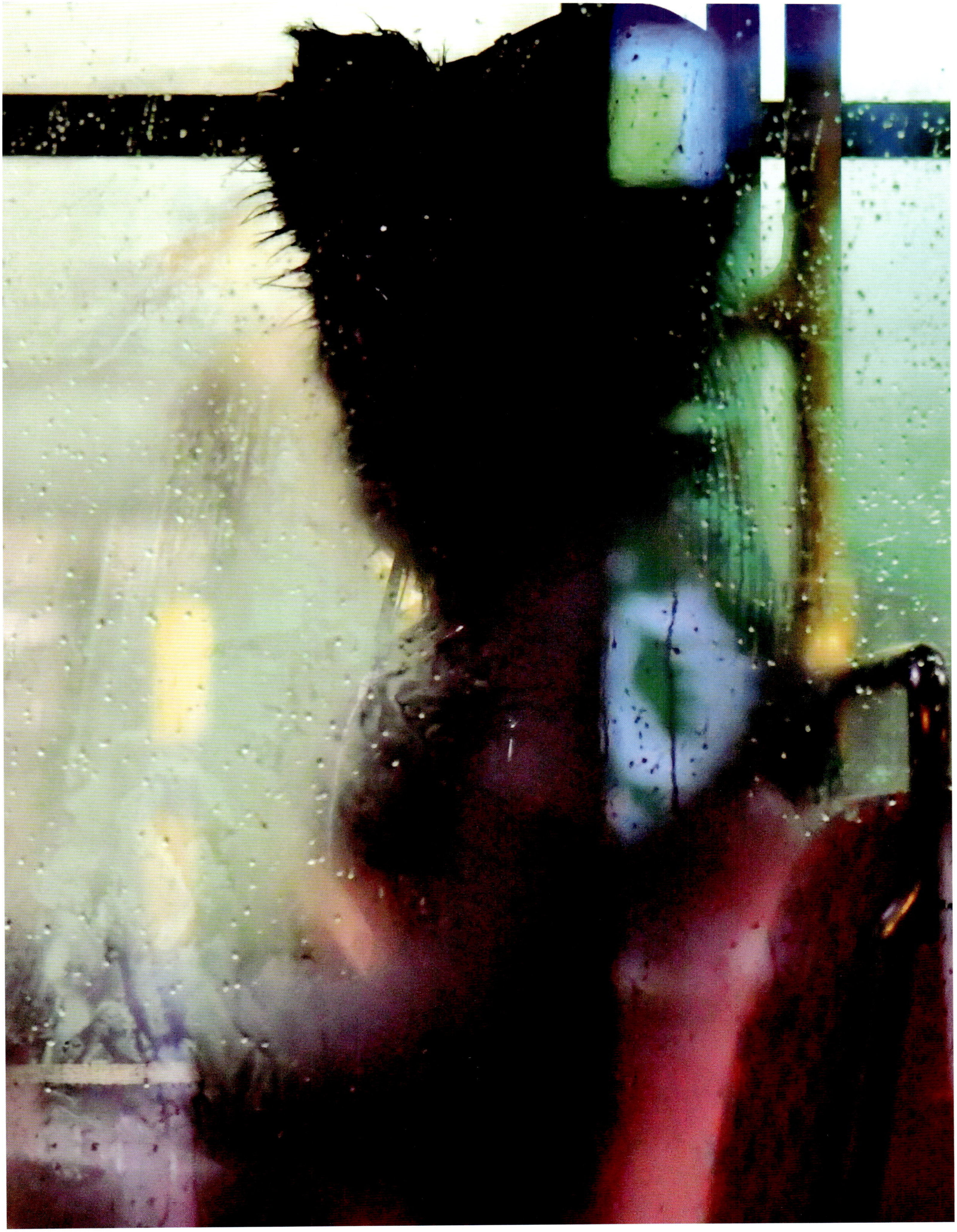

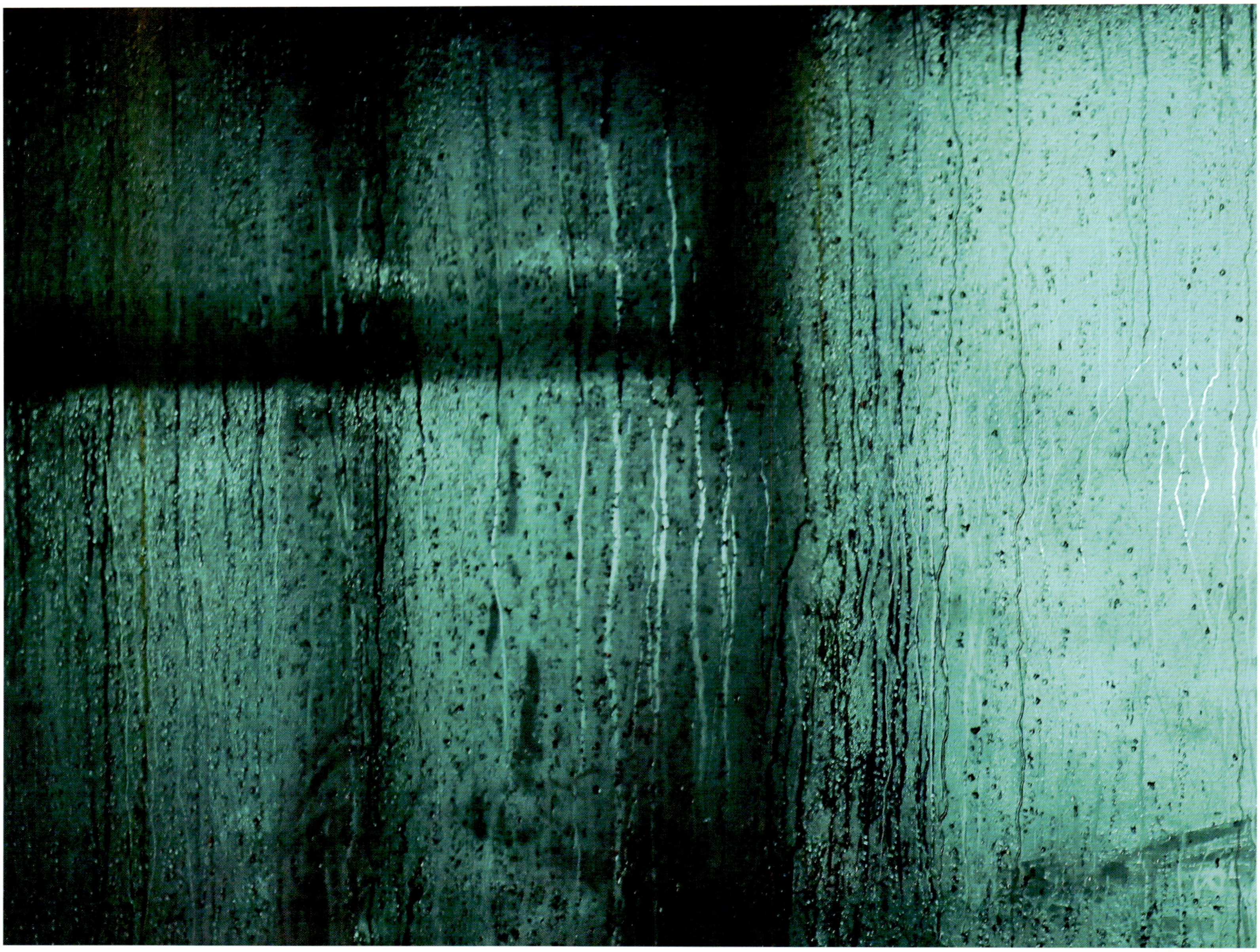

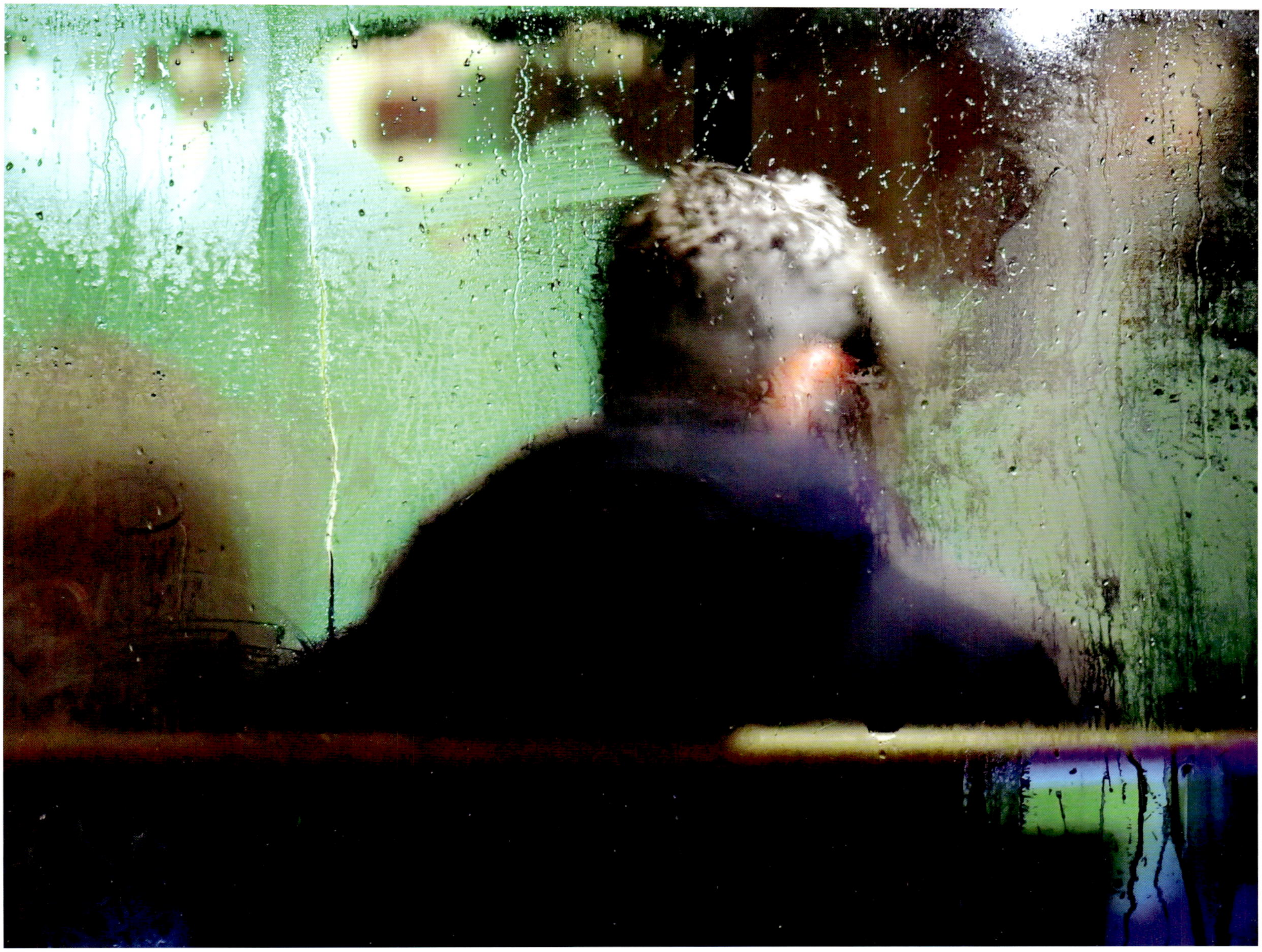

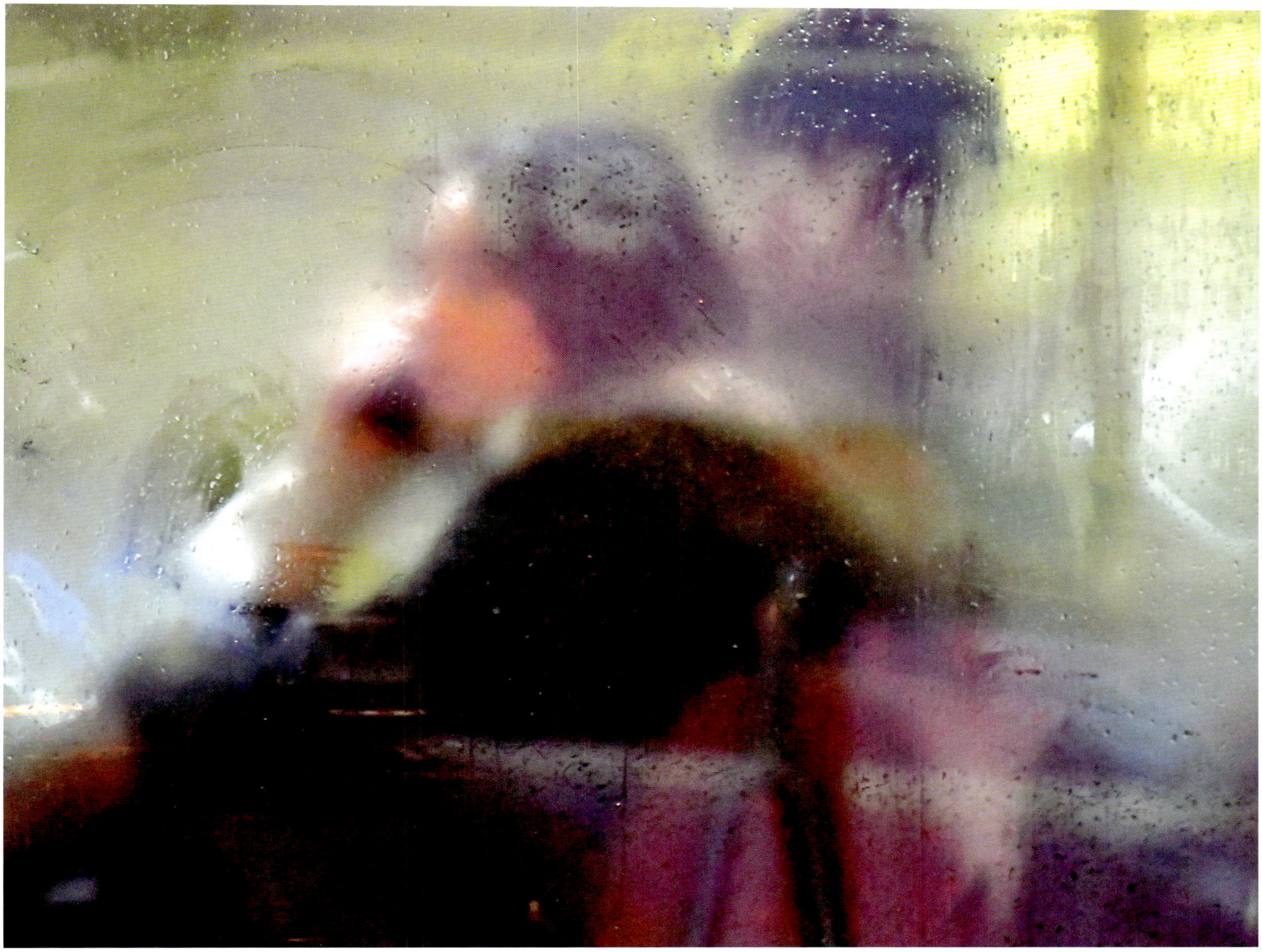

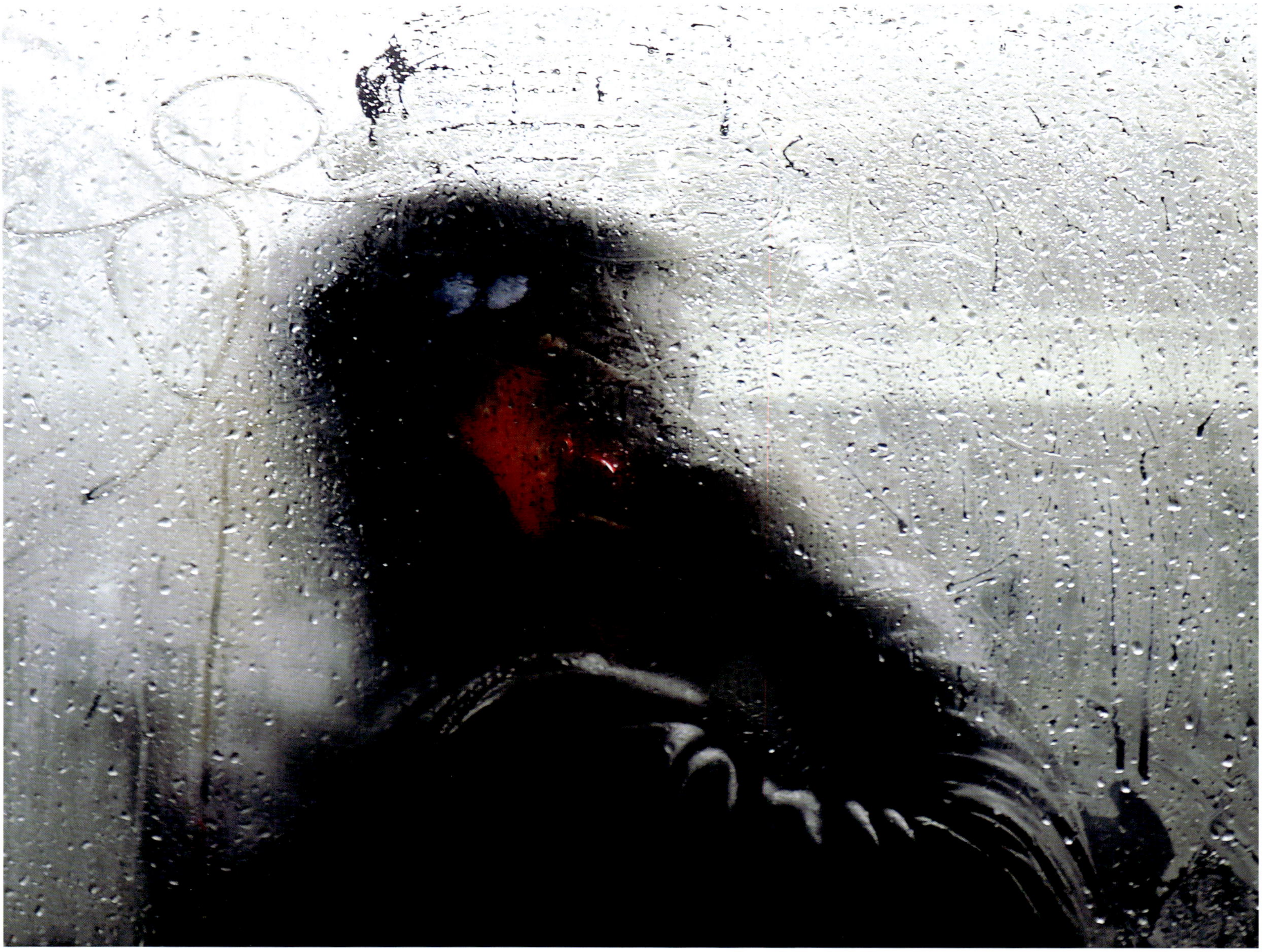

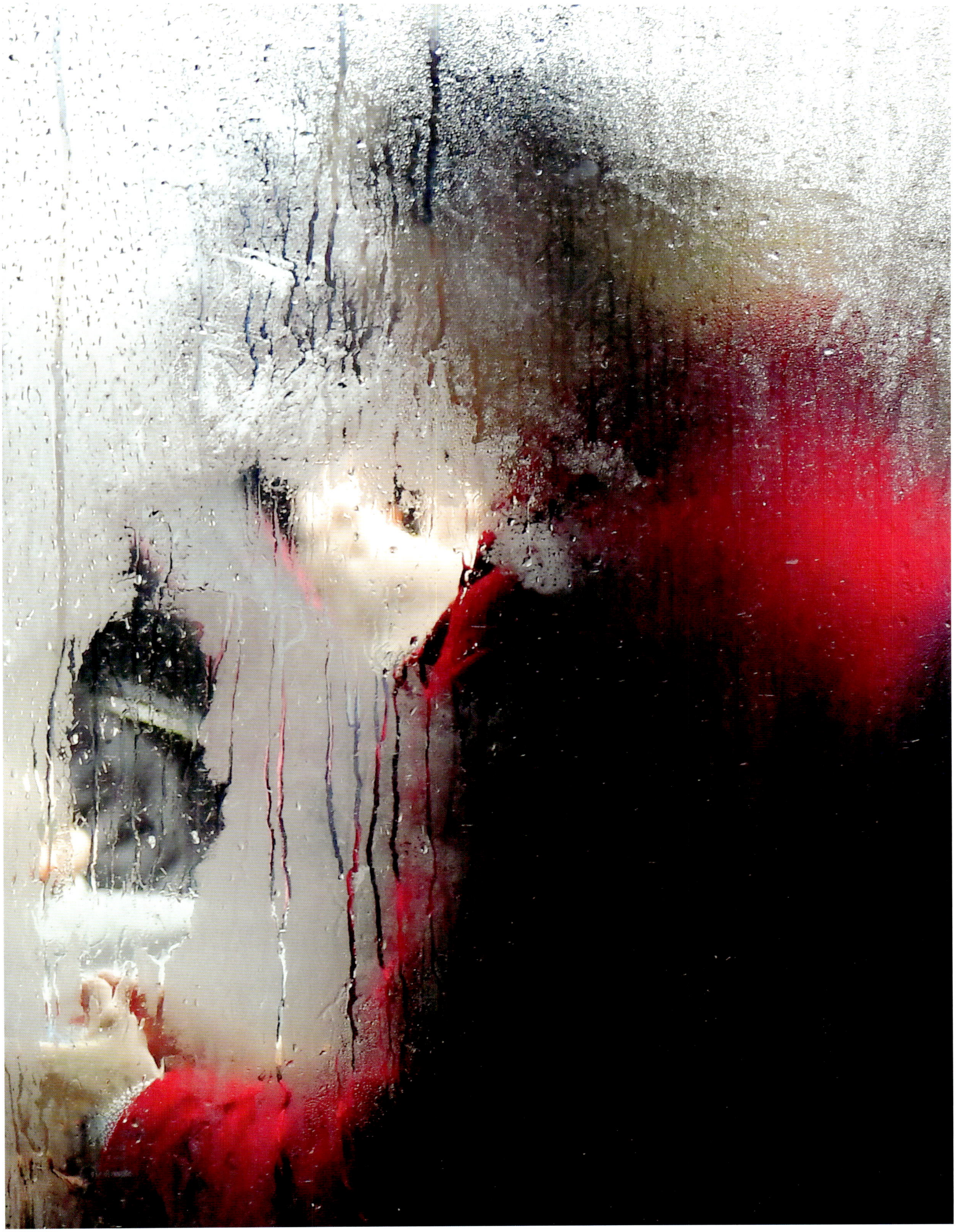

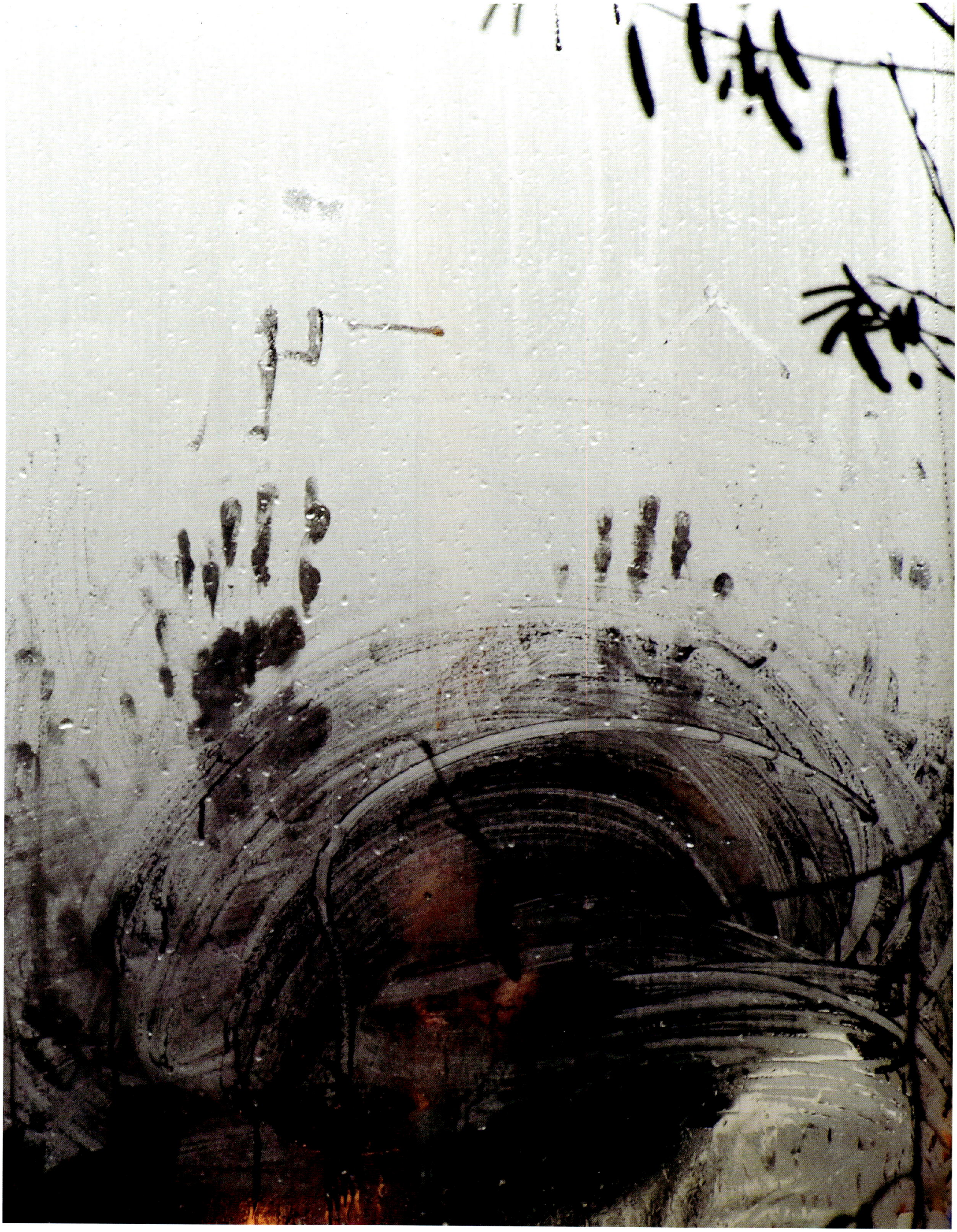

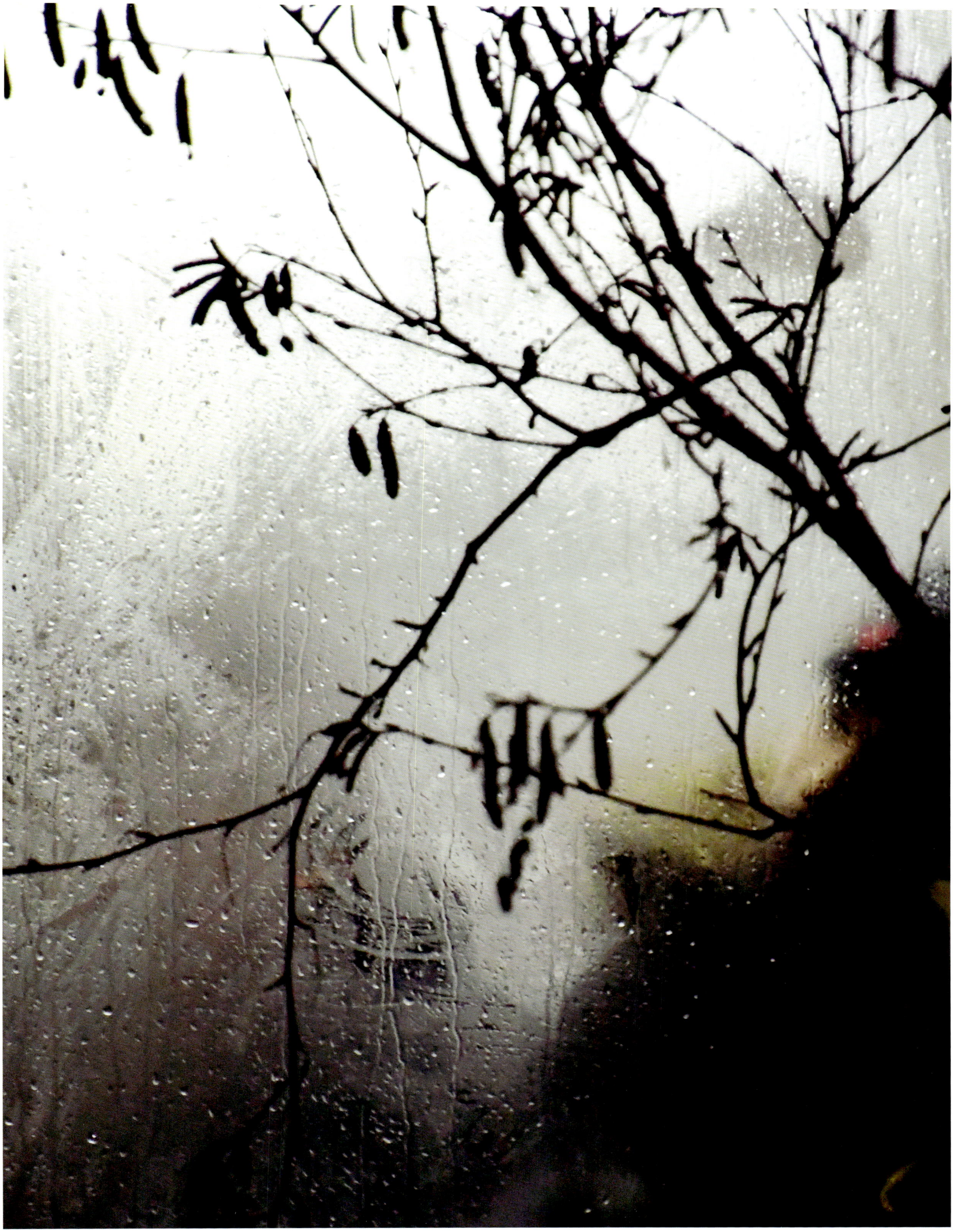

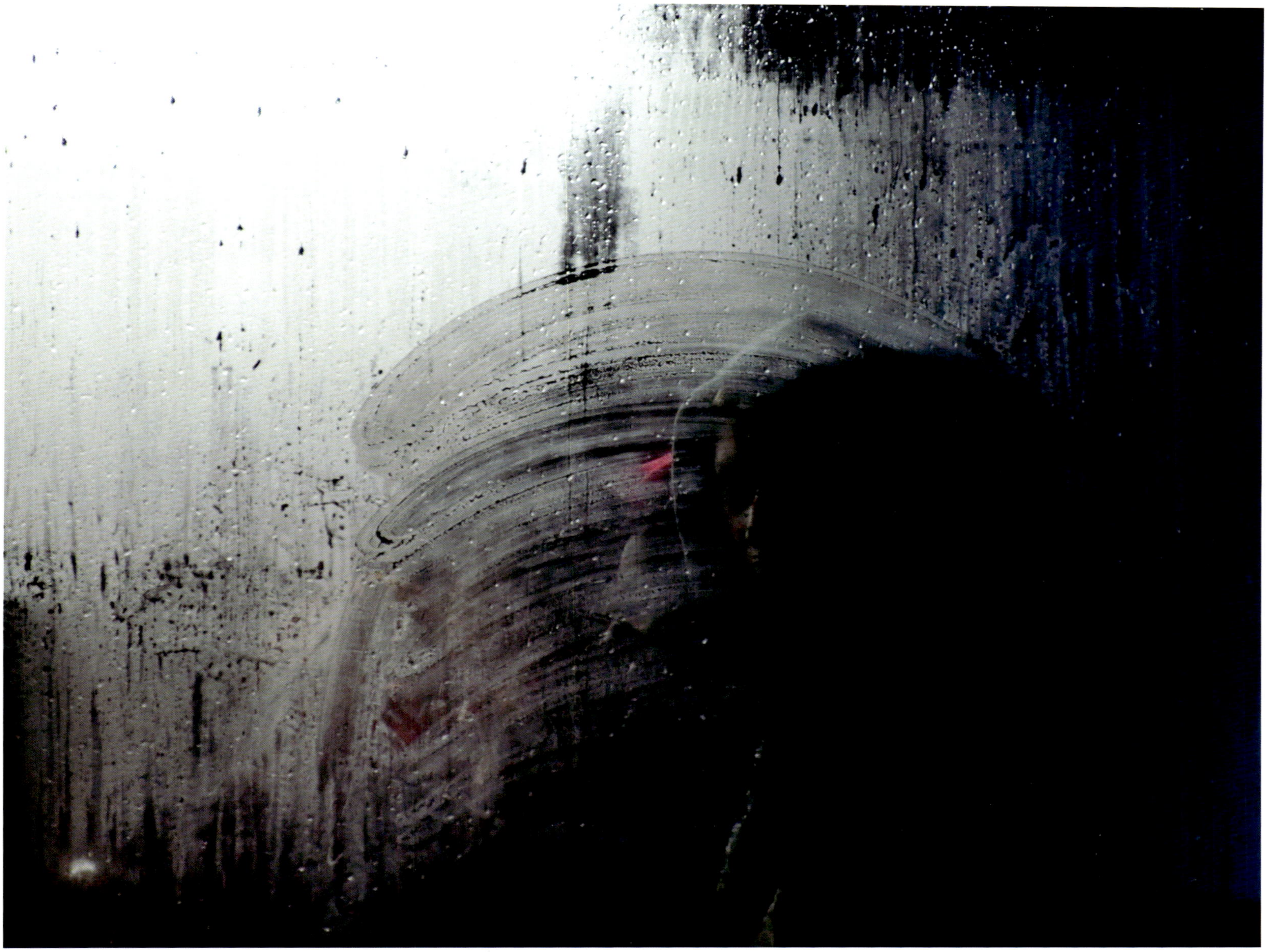

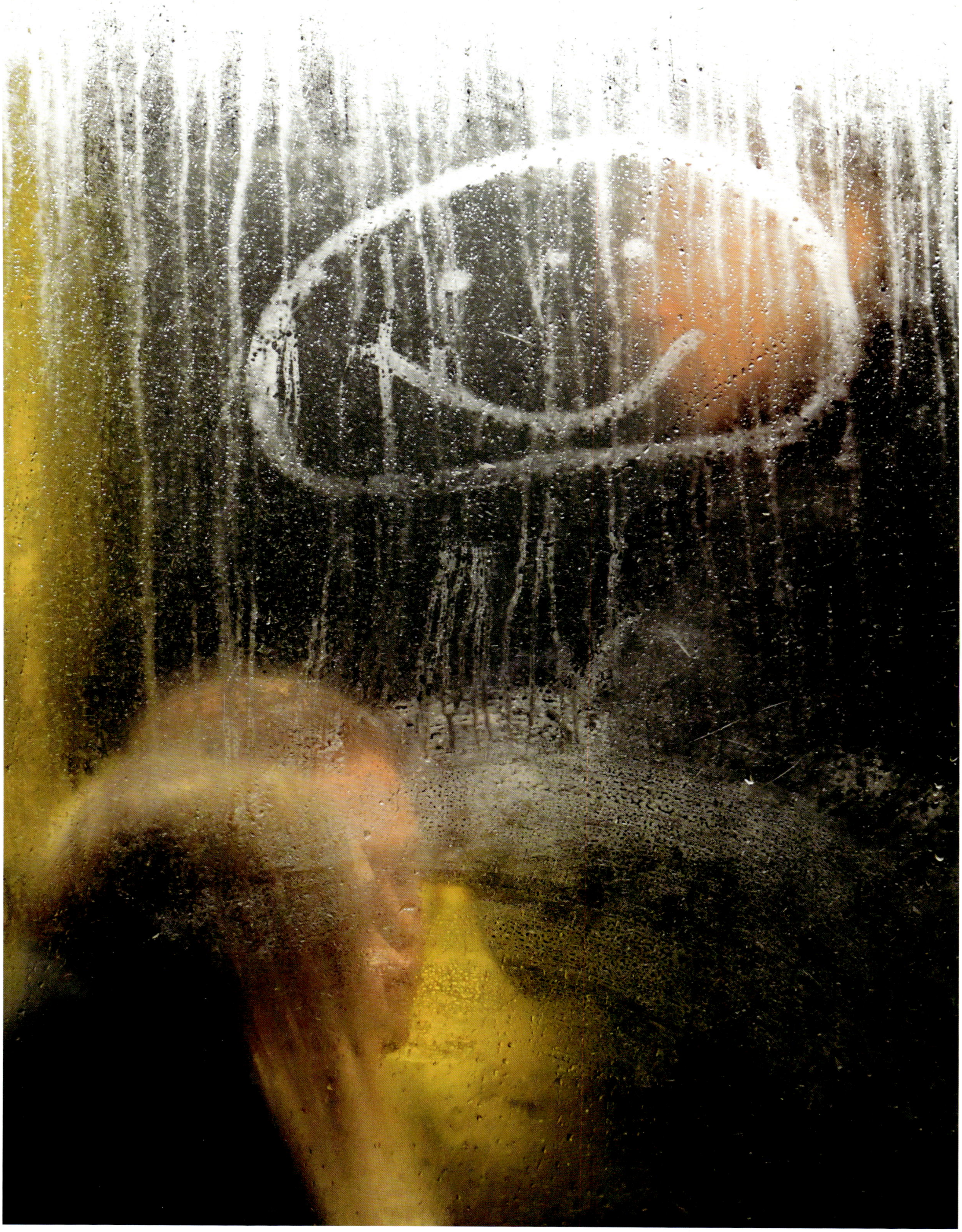

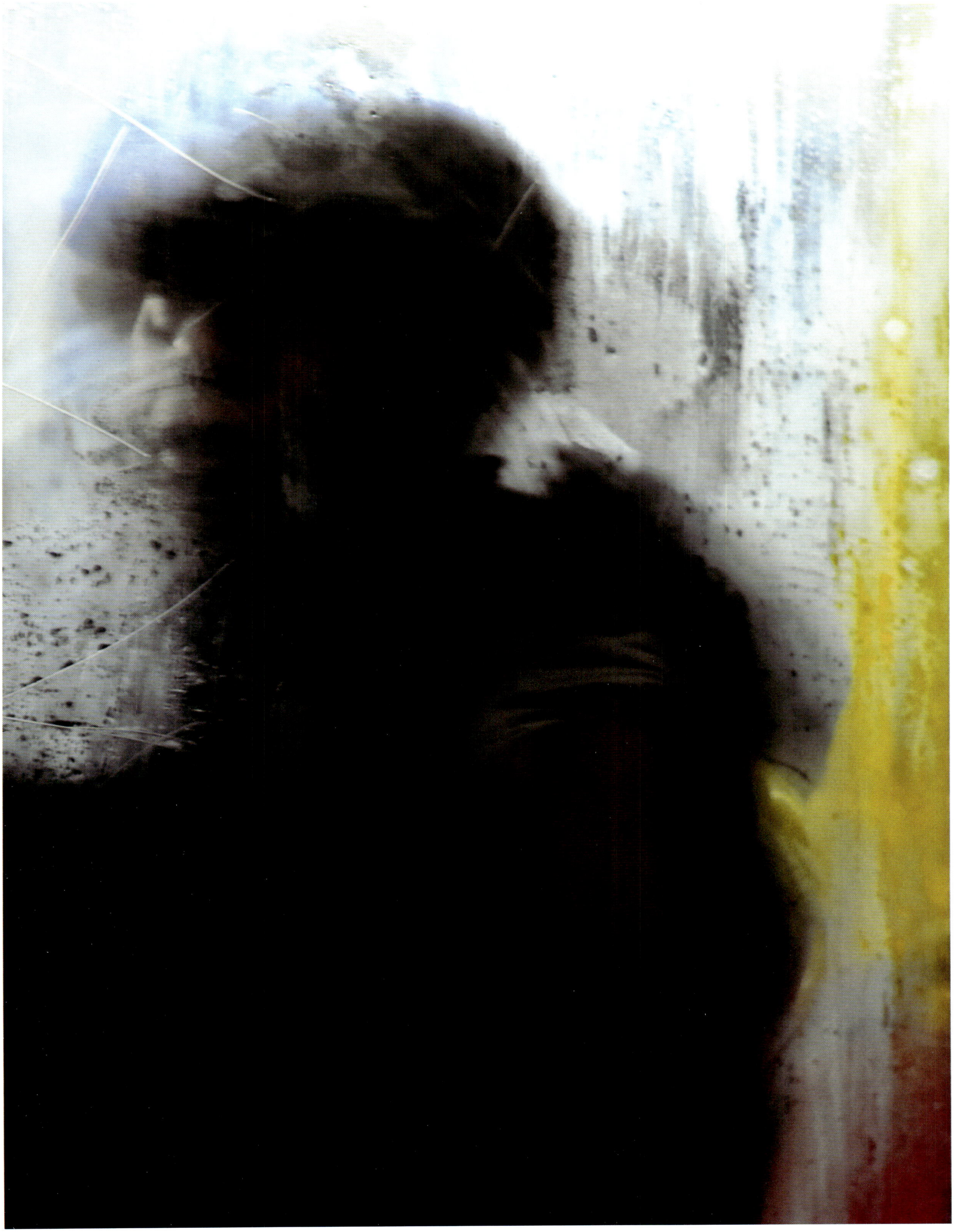

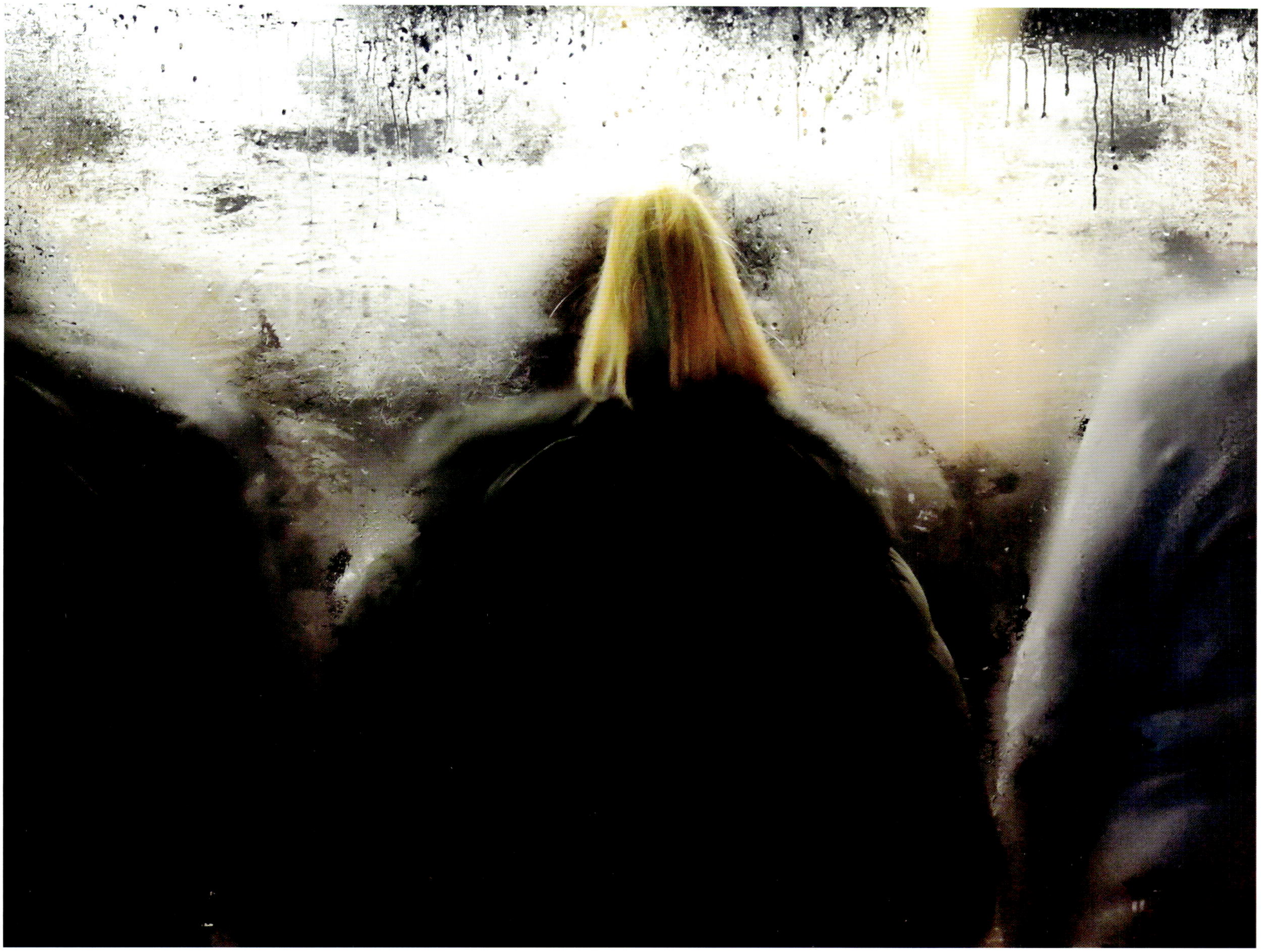

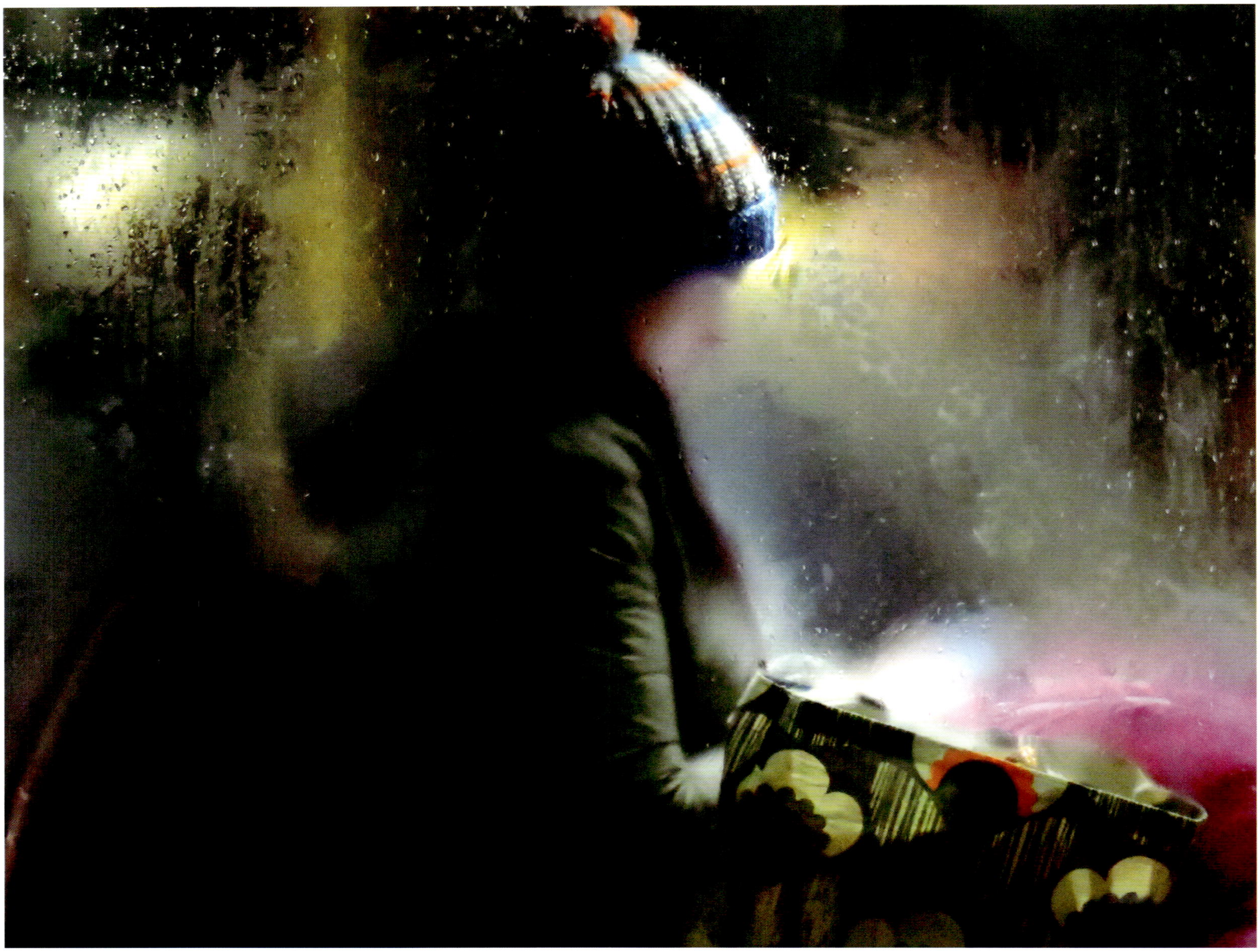

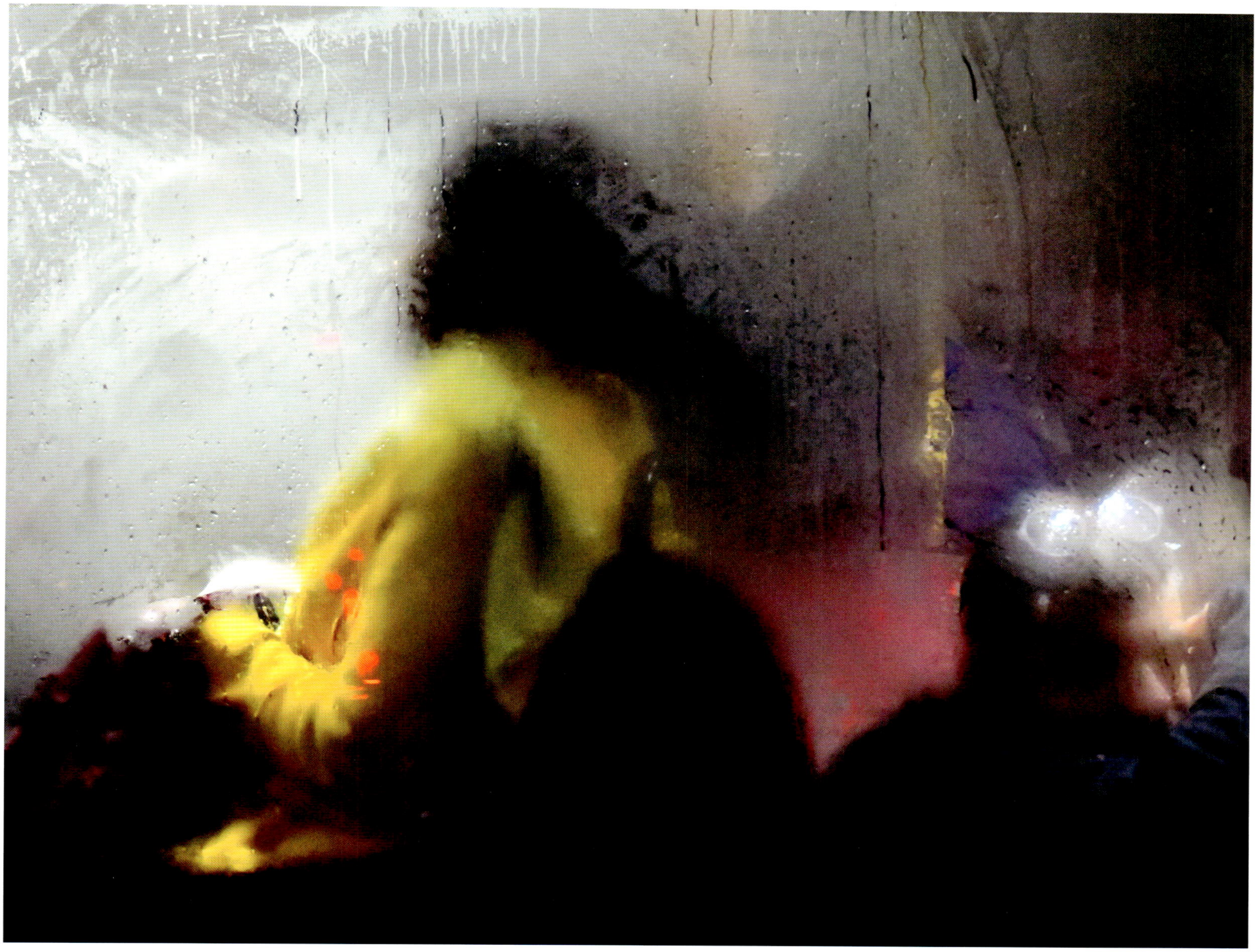

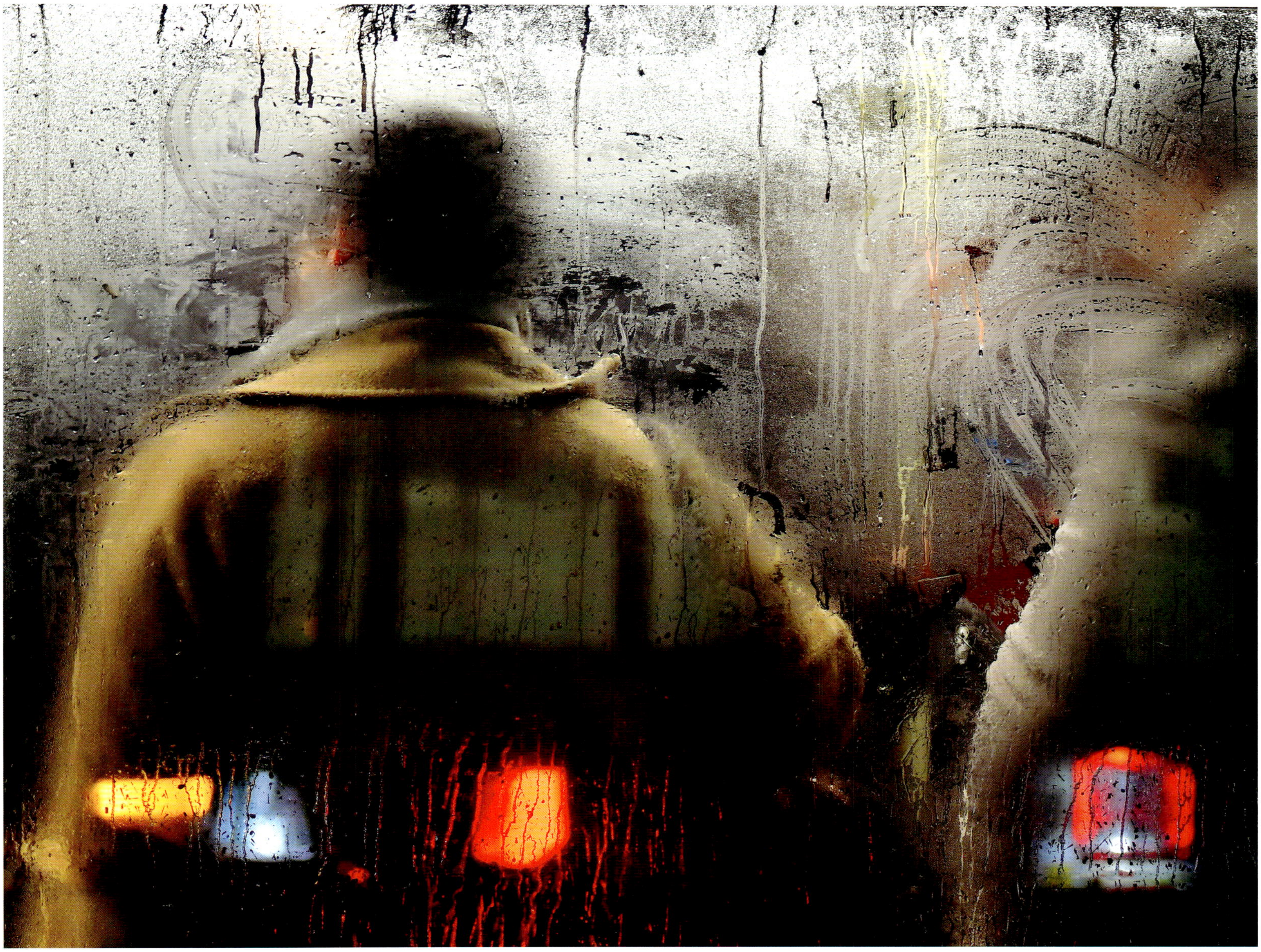

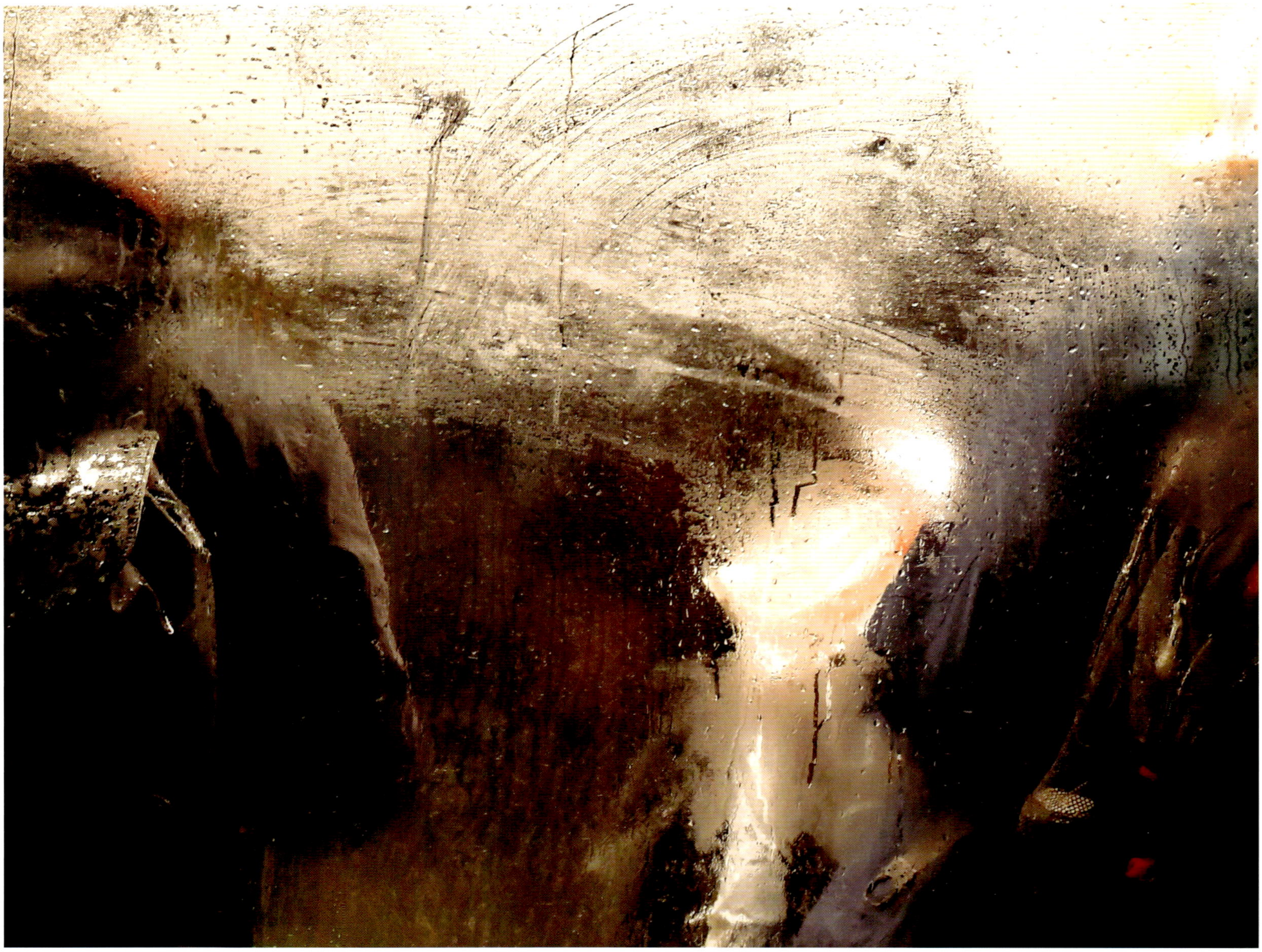

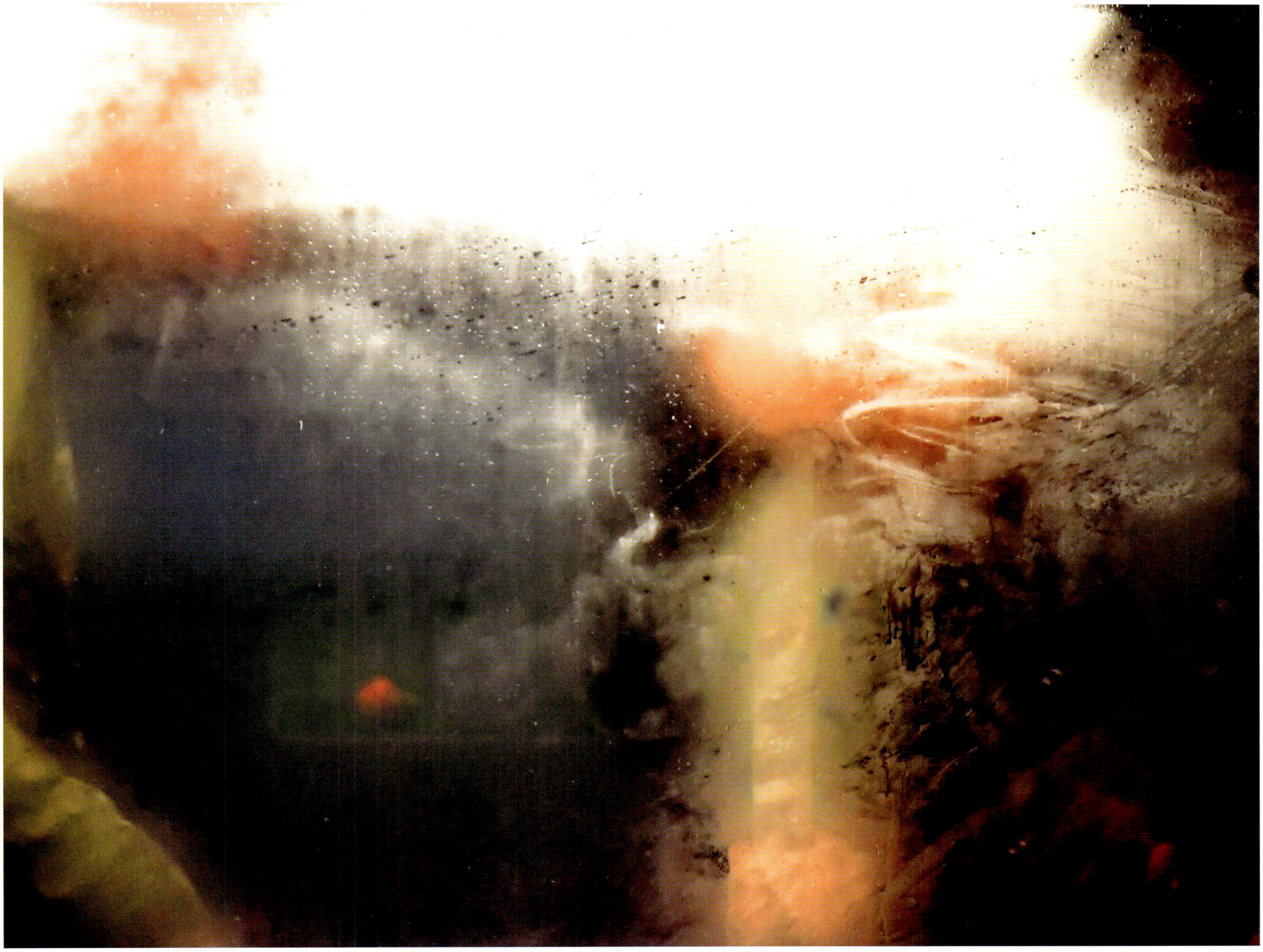

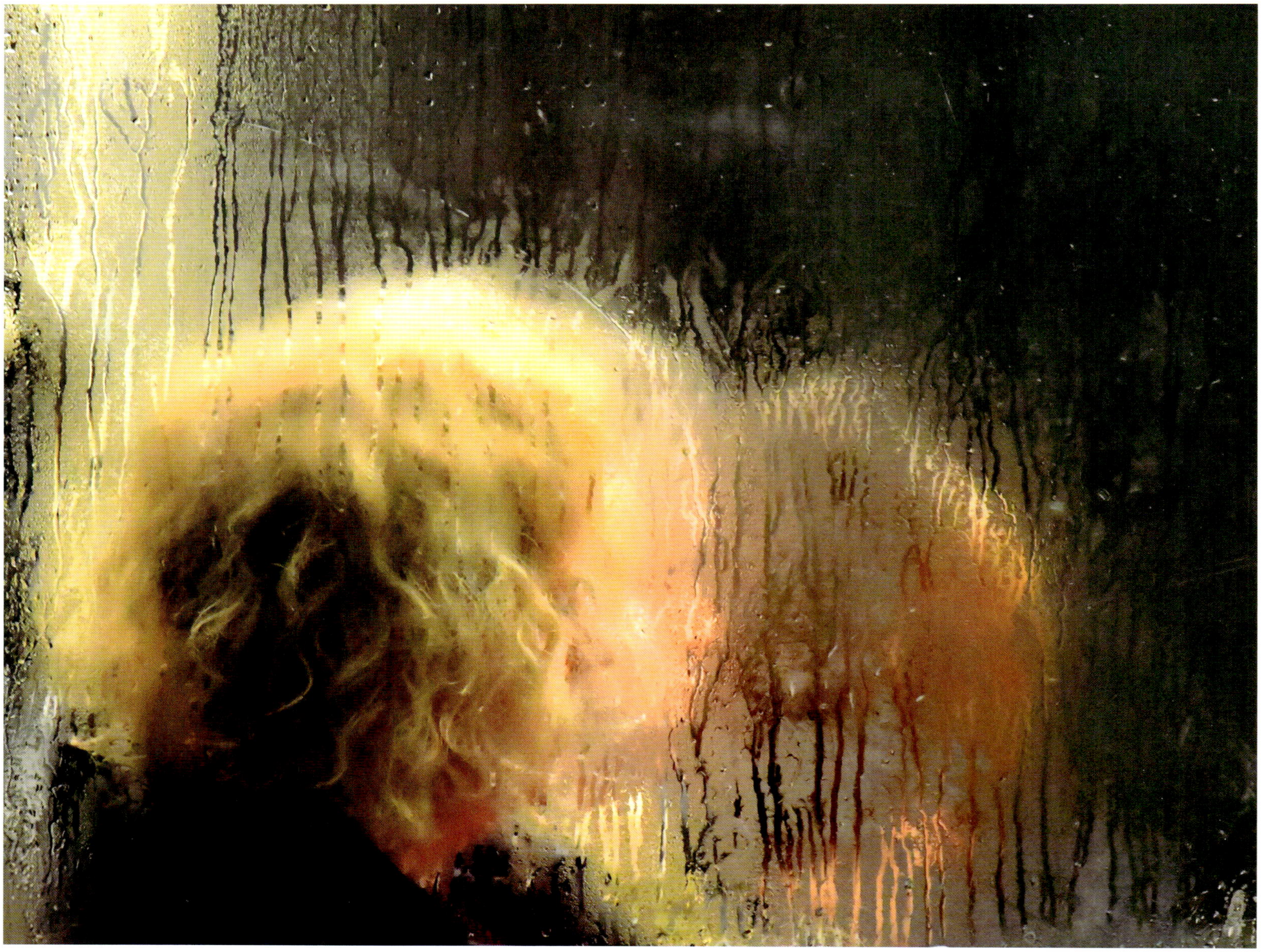

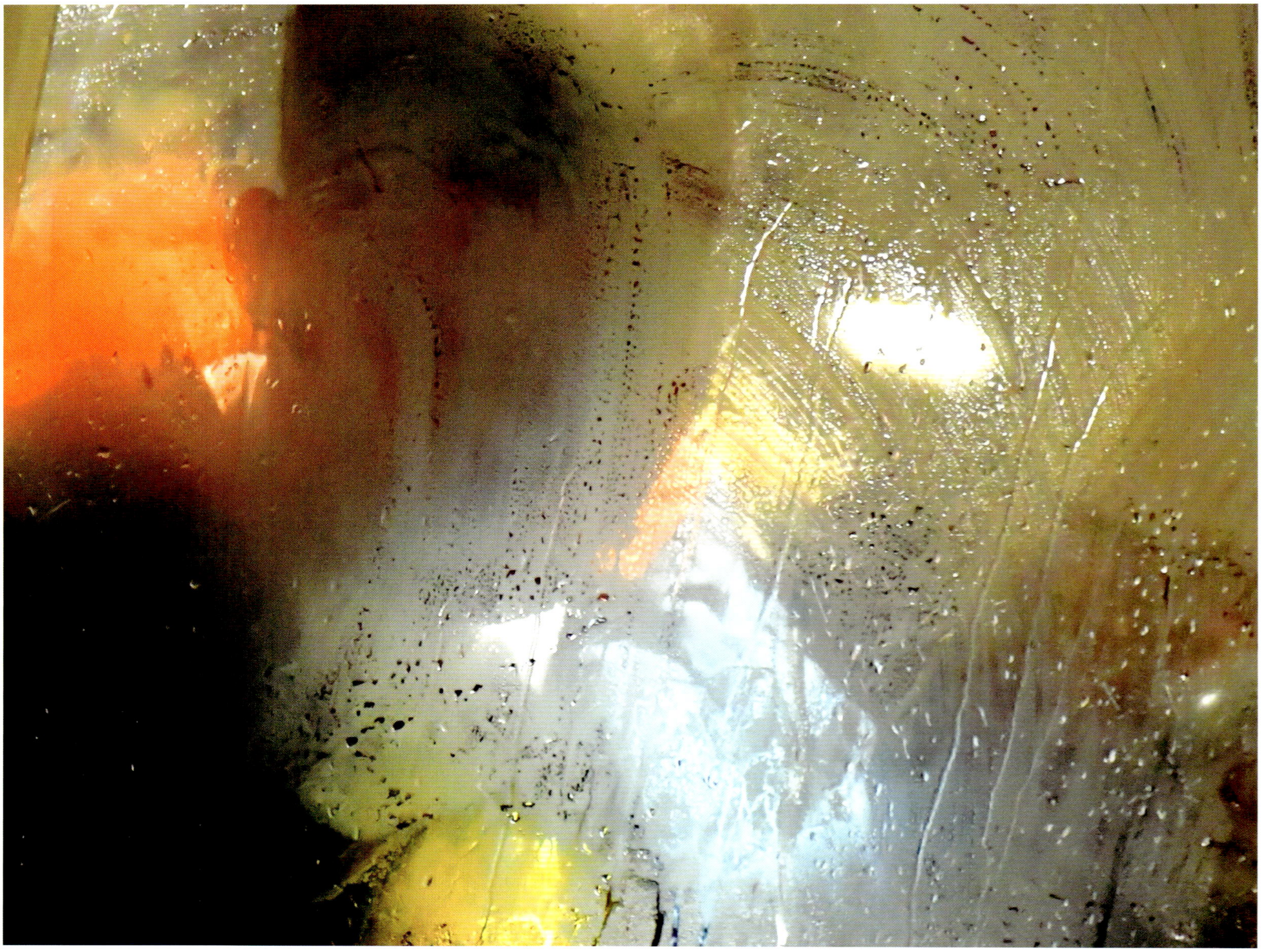

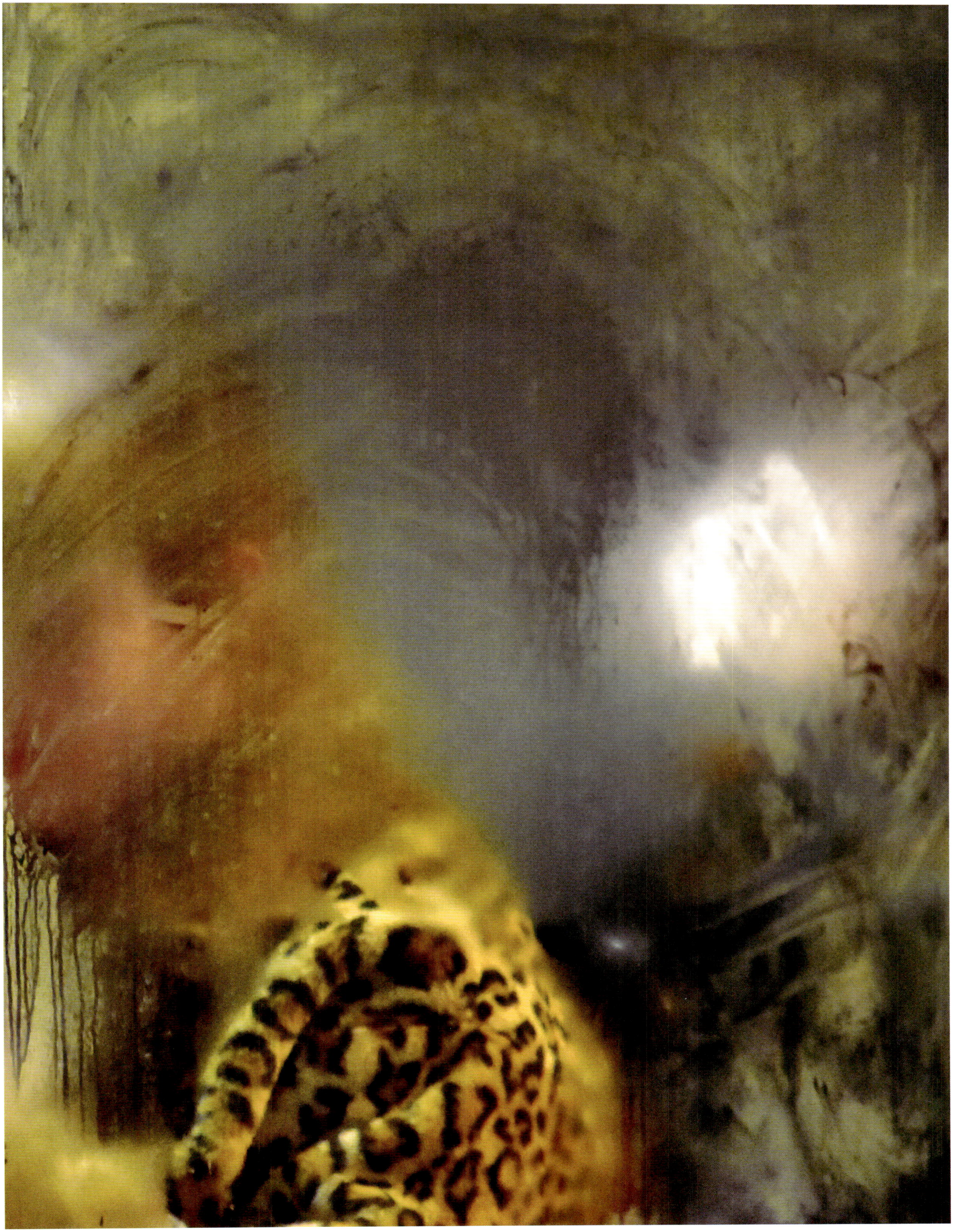

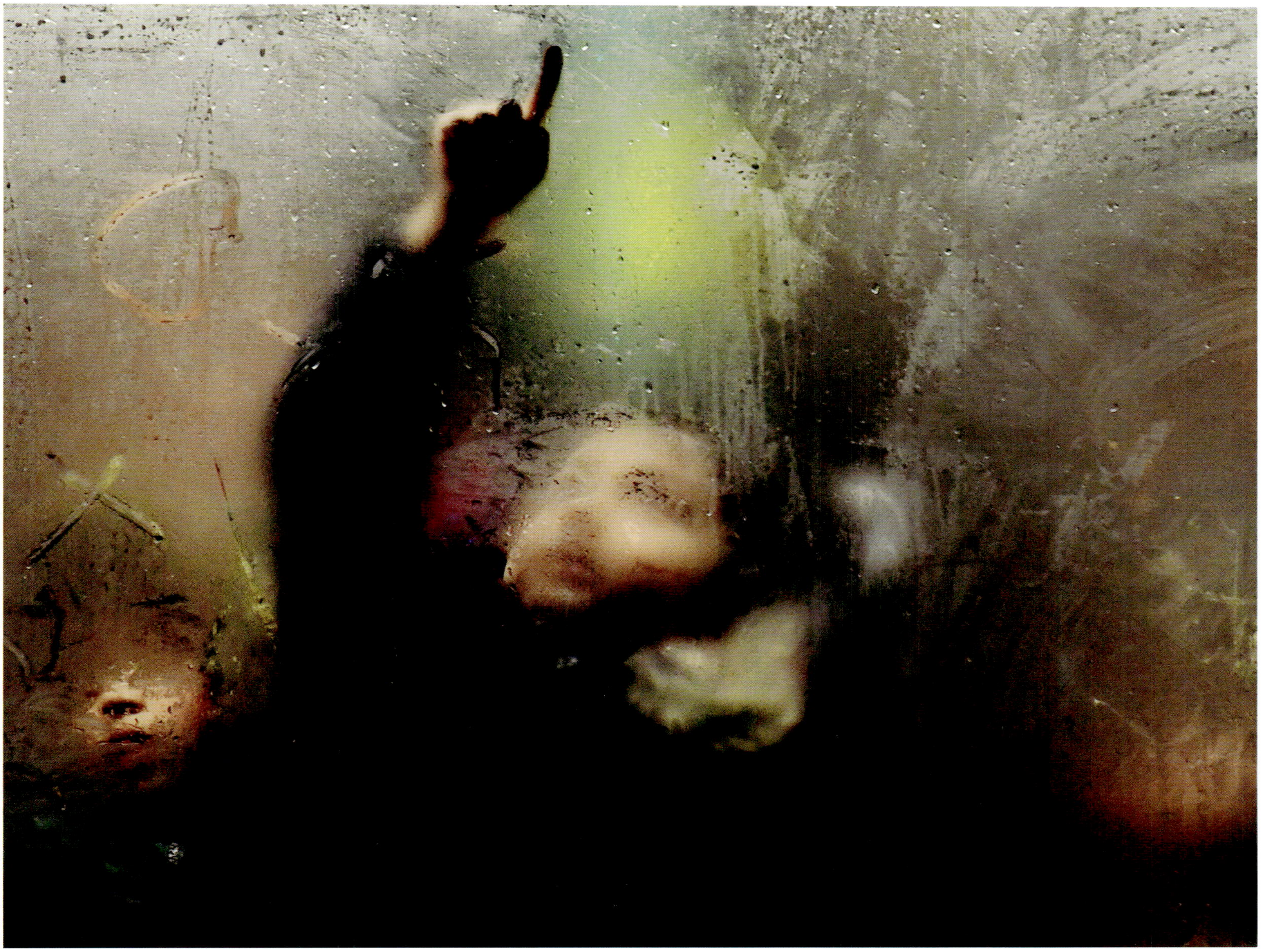

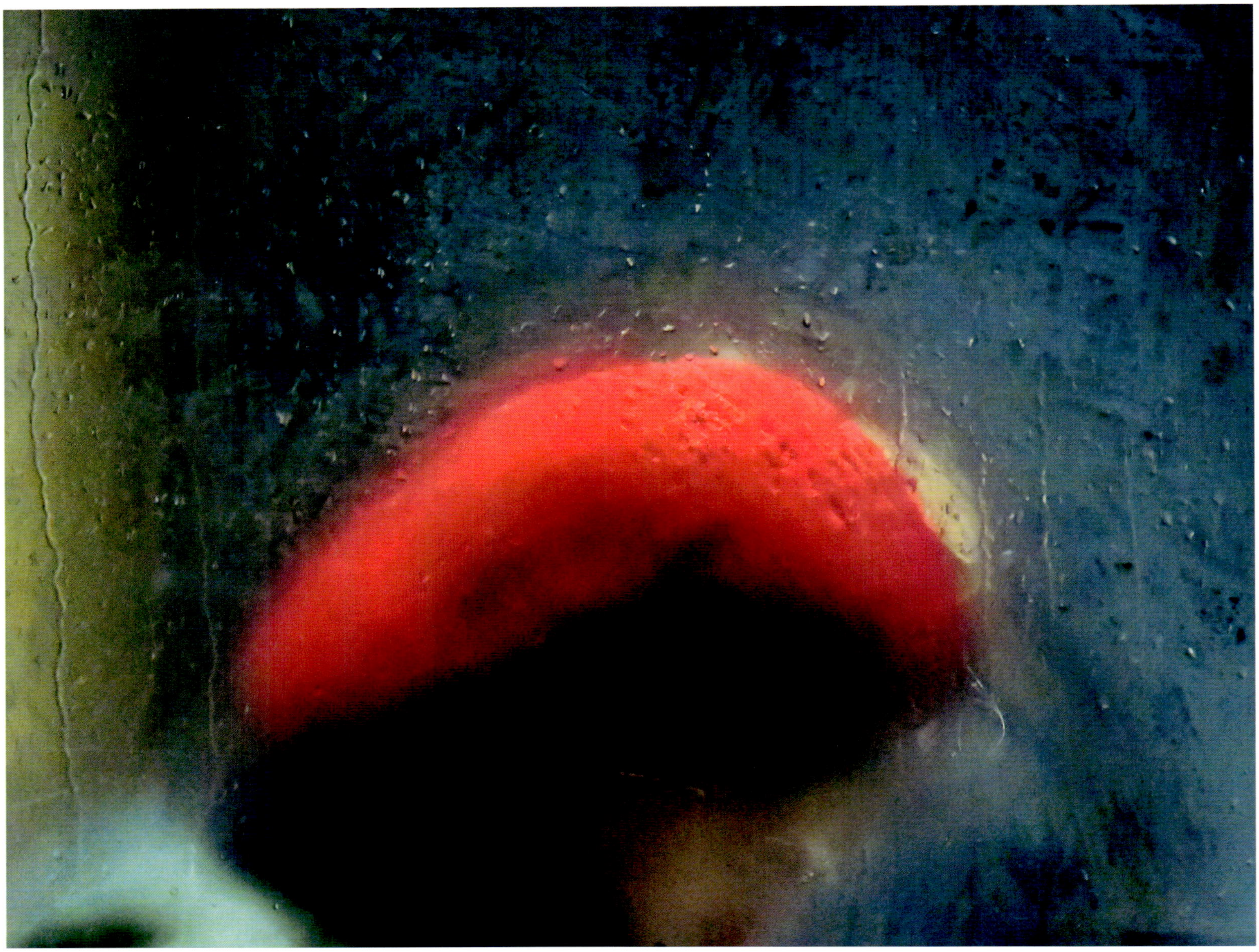

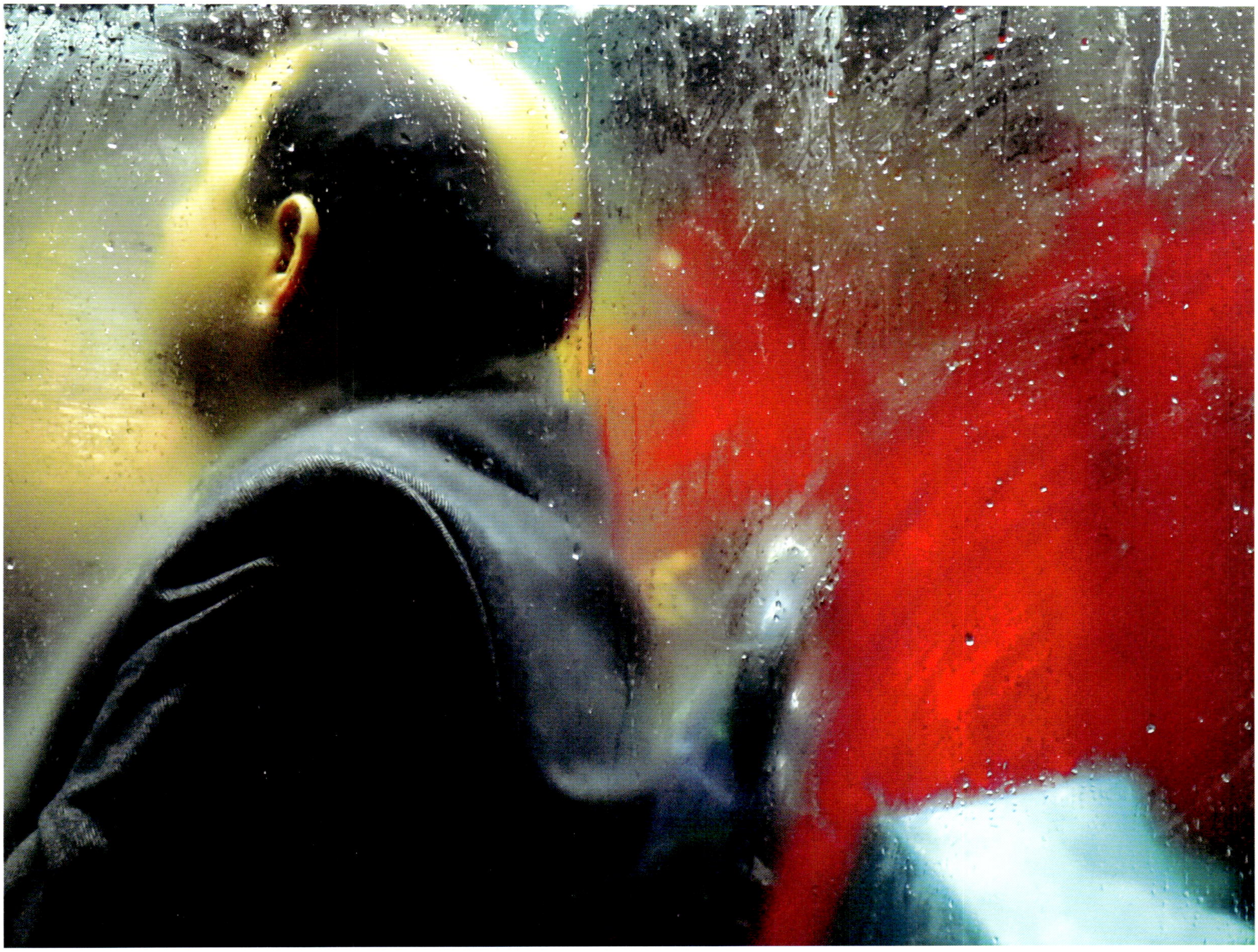

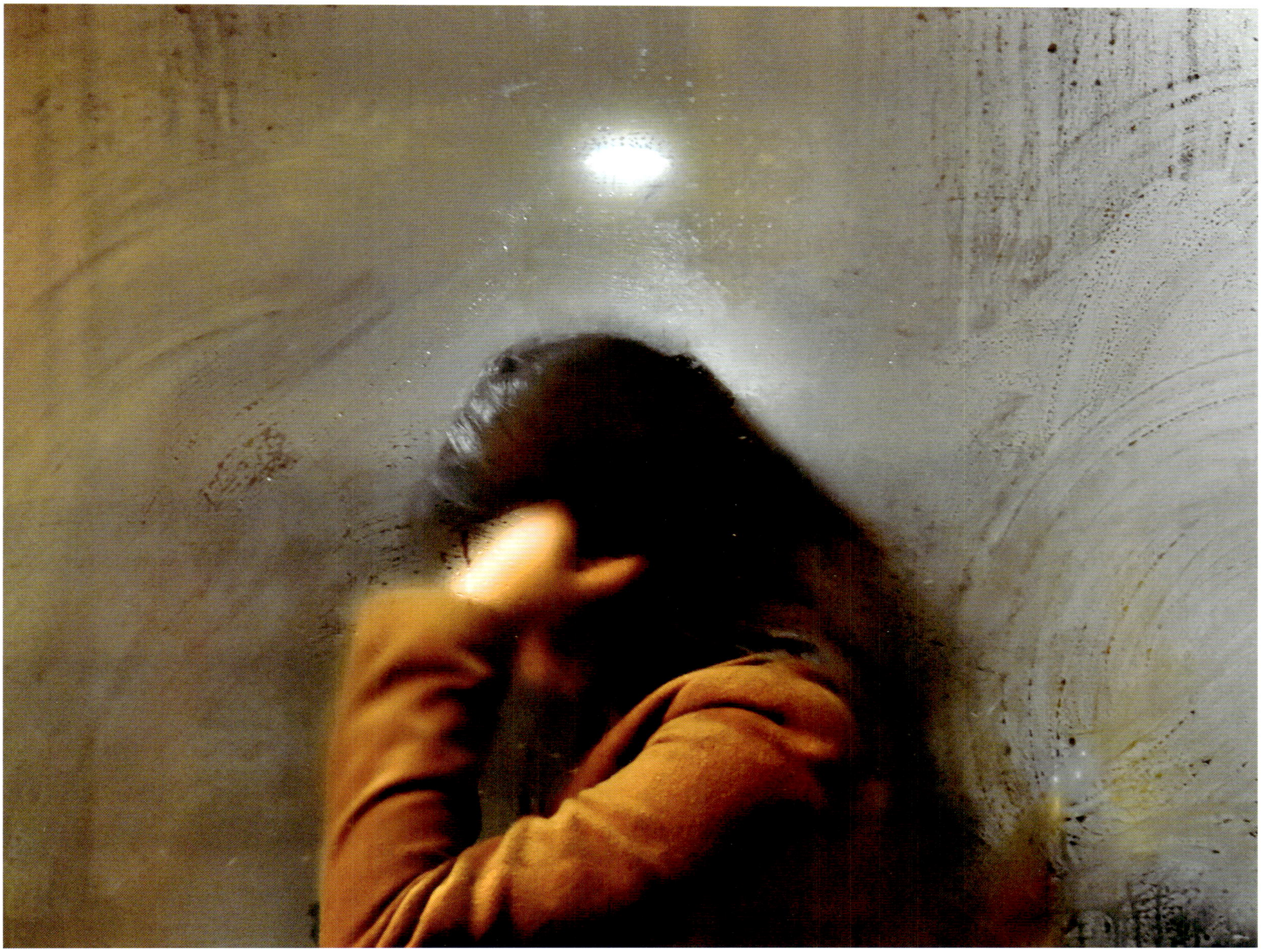

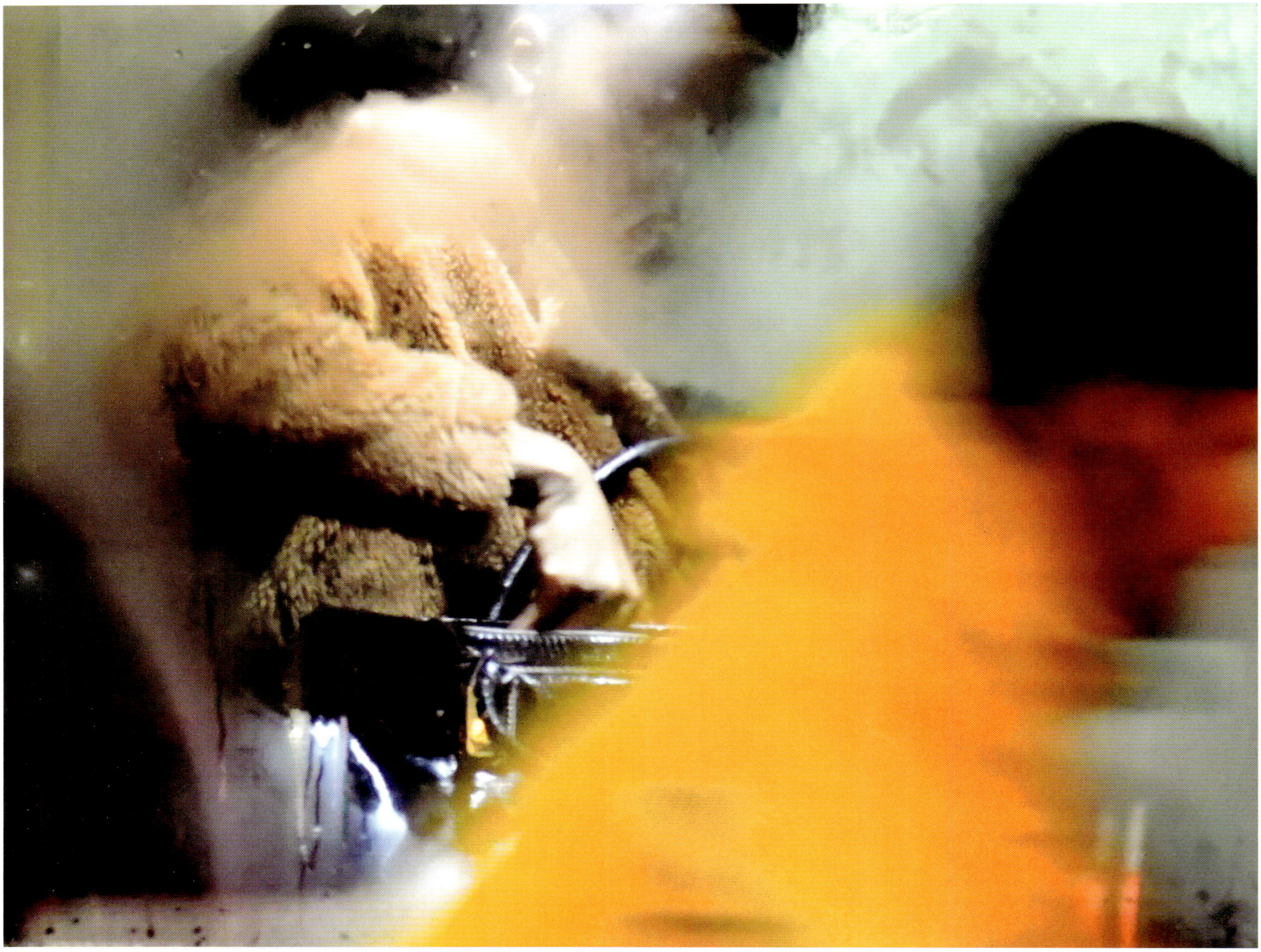

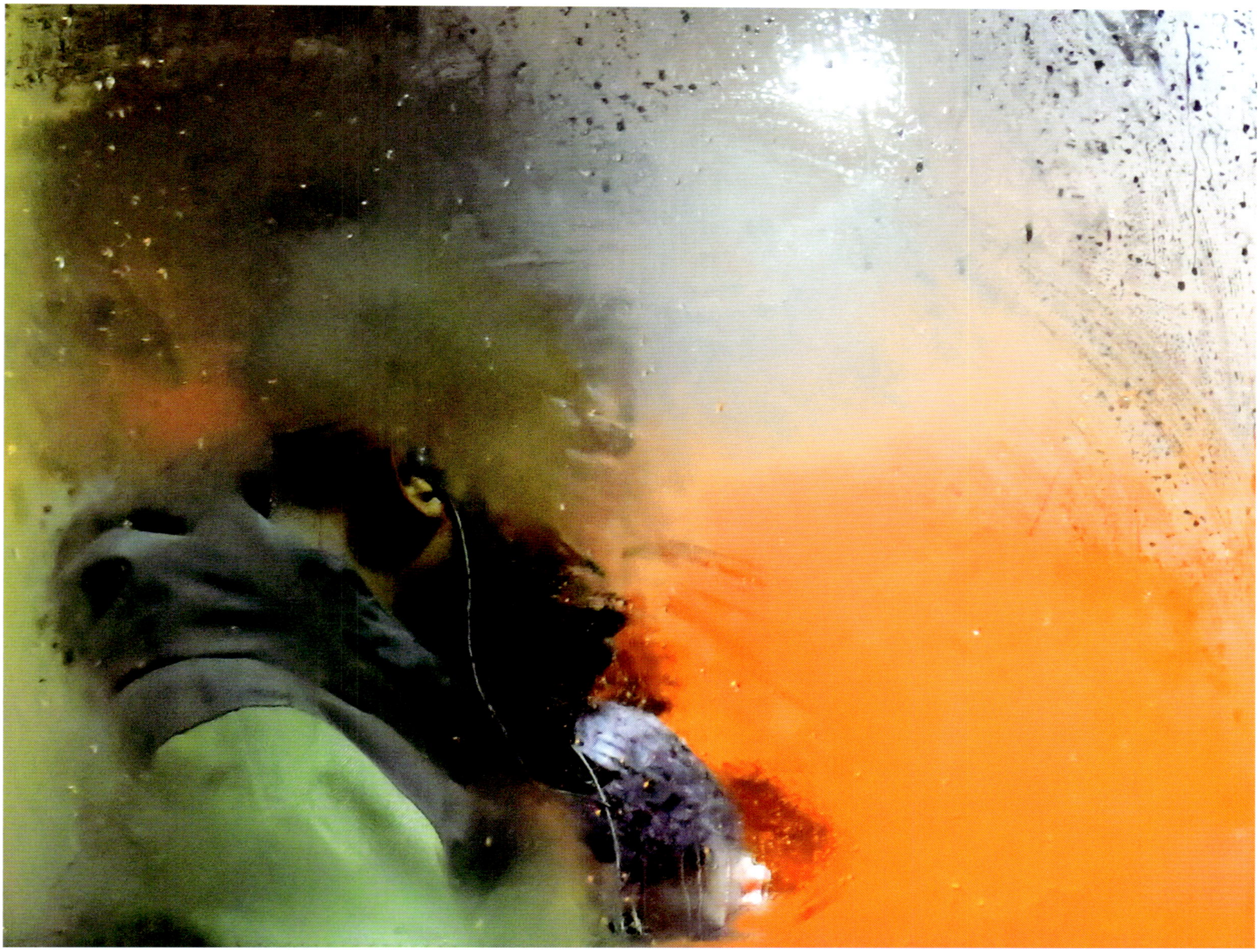

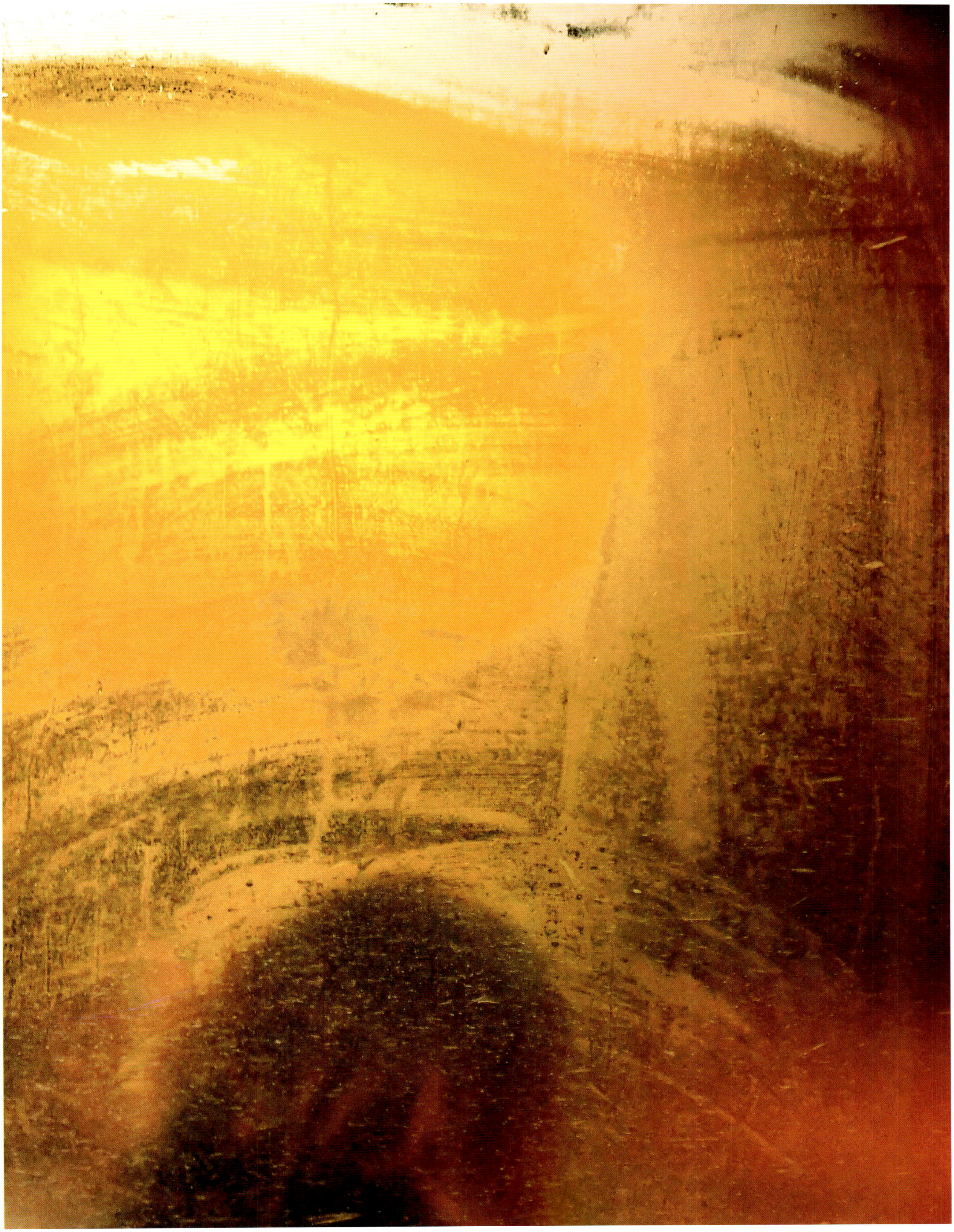

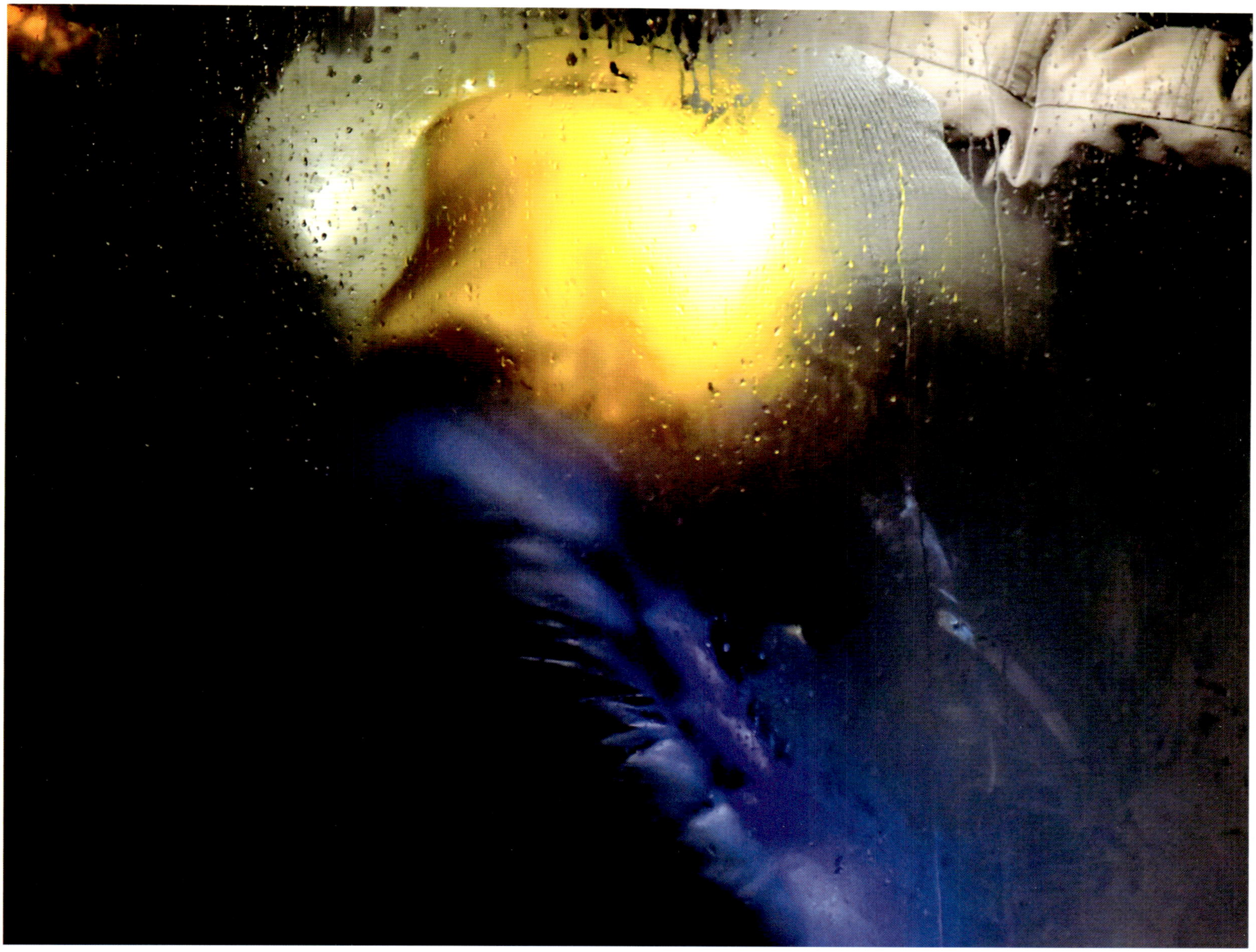

These pictures were made between January 2017 and March 2020, at various locations across London. The vast majority were at Hounslow, Islington, Kingston, Strand, Waterloo and Whitechapel.

This book is dedicated to the memory of my dear parents, Maureen and Ernie. Without them, none of this…

Heartfelt thanks to Denny, Thomas and Christy and the wider family for their endless patience and understanding. And to friends too numerous to mention, whose kind words about my work have sustained and encouraged me—you know who you are.

Particular thanks to the following individuals, for their helpful observations and advice: Martin Parr, Max Pinckers, Mark Power, Fiona Rogers, Nicola Shipley, Stuart Smith and especially Larry Towell. Larry, your timely intervention changed my life; I'm forever in your debt.

This book is a testament to the skills of Stuart Smith and his amazing team at GOST.

Most of all, thanks to the endlessly fascinating, anonymous bus passengers of London, without whom there would be no book.

The GRIND
First published in 2024
by GOST Books, London

info@gostbooks.com
gostbooks.com

Edited and designed by GOST:
Rossella Castello, Katie Clifford, Gemma Gerhard, Justine Hucker, Allon Kaye, Eleanor Macnair, Claudia Paladini, Ana Rocha

Printed in Italy by EBS

British Library cataloguing-in-publication data.
A catalogue record of this book is available from the British Library.

ISBN 978-1-915423-73-3